# Another Round at The Bar

# Another Round at The Bar

Exam Prep Supplement

# CURTIS L. HOWARD JR. ESQ

## SACRAMENTO 2018

Cover:
Curtis L. Howard Jr.
Nathan Fisher
Danielle Varner

Howard Jr., Curtis
Another Round at The Bar: a repeat taker's guide to
success / Curtis L. Howard Jr., Sacramento: 2018

ISBN: 978-1-945526-24-4

Library of Congress Control Number: 2017919504

Manufactured in the United States of America

I Street Press
828 I Street
Sacramento, CA 95814

# Table of Contents

PREFACE .........................................................................iv

ABOUT THE AUTHOR.....................................................x

HOW TO USE THIS BOOK............................................ xiii

Clean Slate..................................................................3

Making an Honest Self-Assessment ......................... 17

Reassessing Your Exam ............................................ 39

Accepting the Challenge........................................... 85

Setting the Mind..................................................... 102

Perfect Practice Makes Perfect .............................. 135

The Groundhog Day Effect ...................................... 160

SELECTED DIARY ENTRIES........................................ 169

SPECIAL THANKS..................................................... 177

# Dedication
*Flora Pierce Williams*

# PREFACE

## A law school graduate walks into a bar...

If you're reading this book, then you probably have taken a professional exam and not passed or taken an entrance exam and didn't earn a high enough score to get you into the school of your choice. But, you are a person who thinks ahead and are anticipating your next licensing exam soon. You are reading this book for a heads-up to help you avoid the pitfalls that lead to becoming a repeat taker. I'd like you to take a moment to congratulate yourself for your perseverance. Why? I'm sure you are aware of some your peers who have taken their licensing exam and did not pass and as a result have given up. You on the other hand are continuing to take the necessary steps to achieve your goal and that deserves an applause.

The journey as a repeat taker can be alienating and lonely but I can assure you that, "You are not alone..." Sing!!! "I am here with you." Ok, ok cut it, before I receive a cease and desist from the Jackson estate. I took the California State Bar five times before passing. One, two, three, four, five. 1, 2, 3, 4, 5, uno, dos, tres, quarto, cinco. Did you cringe after reading that? How do you think I feel when I tell people?

Well surprise, I feel fine about it. And the quick fix to patch up any hard feelings you have about taking your professional exam multiple times is to simply own it. I'm not suggesting that you go shouting the number of times you took your exam from the top of Mount Everest. But it is a number you are going to live with for the rest of your career, so you want to focus on the positive effects of being a repeat taker. After all, repeating the exam is an odyssey all its own and an opportunity for personal growth.

Since you are privy to the wonders of multiple exam administrations you might as well use it to your advantage. What advantages you ask? Well, I chose to write a book! I'd matured so much as a person during my rounds with the Bar that I wanted to share my experience with others. I needed a way to cope with the undeniable fact that I was a repeat taker and I wanted to shake off the stigma associated with it. I set out to prove to myself and to anyone doubting their worth or intelligence as a repeat taker that not only can you pass, but you can also use the experience as a creative catalyst. This is the process of turning a perceived negative into a tangible positive.

After passing the Bar, offers from big firms didn't come pouring in. Not that I'd planned to be a corporate lawyer but even my original plan of working for a California county public defender's office hadn't panned out. So, I started a solo criminal law practice. In the beginning, it was tough getting enough clients to pay all the bills and make a profit, so I decided to get creative and write a book.

For a while I didn't know what type of book to write, but I did know that I wanted to write about something within my personal knowledge. While preparing for the Bar I read several books for both academic purposes and leisure. Some were spiritual texts about Eastern religions like Buddhism and Hara Krishna. I learned to practice meditation, spiritual healing and heightening my focus. Other books had a practical use focusing on technical skills like legal writing and financial planning. After reading these books I felt invigorated. I used my down time between studying to reflect on my character while considering the book I was reading at the time. Through this process, I began to unveil the flaws in my study habits, work ethic, attitude toward being a repeat taker and ultimately life! Then it dawned on me. I would share this experience with others so that they too could learn to endure preparing for their professional exams by learning how to stay positive and be self -motivated.

Writing this book was cathartic. Everyday I'd come up with new ideas, formats, and subject matter then incorporated them into the text as I wrote. I continued to read more books to improve my writing and connect with my audience. I talked to my colleagues about their experiences and wove it into the fabric of the text. The point of my research was to create a book that was more than just my Bar story interlaced with some helpful tips. I wanted to create a tool that could be used in conjunction with any professional exam prep course. So, think of this book as a conversation between old buddies. I'm going to share with you my story with hopes that it gives you a sense of companionship (can you hear the melody? You are not alone. Don't stop singing.) And yes, the book's tone will be somewhat informal and cheeky at times, but that's because I want you to lighten up so that you can enjoy preparing for your next exam. After you have passed your professional exam you will quickly see that you can have a thriving career and your professional community will value what you offer despite the number of times you took the Bar exam.

Although this book uses my experience with the California State Bar as the context to illustrate how and why my philosophy worked for me, it is also useful if you are taking other professional licensing exams as well. To start your preparation off strongly you must work to get into a passing mindset no matter the test you are taking. Also, you may be thinking, "I already have a positive disposition, I don't need to change my mindset." If that is the case, great! Then think of this book as a refresher, a piece of exercise equipment that will strengthen what you already know.

For practical purposes, this book is filled with substantive hints and tricks for success at taking the California State Bar. But, if you are looking for a memorable pneumonic for the elements of negligence or a sure-fire way to outline your issues, rules, analysis and conclusions (I.R.A.C) any hypothetical fact pattern then stop reading. This book is not a comprehensive outline. Your focus will be on creating a mindset that welcomes the challenges associated with thorough preparation. This book will have quotable quotes and exercises that can realign your *chakras* for a positive disposition when times are at their worst. I'd suggest you finish reading this book before you start studying for your next attempt. Then, **keep it handy** and periodically reference the quotable quotes to keep your spirits up. **Use a highlighter** to illuminate the tricks and tips throughout the chapters you think compliment your preparation. Thus, the lessons you learn in this book will help you create a more positive outlook on being a repeat taker and will be with you for the rest of your life.

Most of this book was written when the California State Bar Examination was a three-day exam. Effective July 2017 the General Bar will be a two-day examination, consisting of three parts: five essay questions, the Multistate Bar Examination (MBE), and one performance test (PT). The parts of the examination may not be taken separately, and California does not accept the transfer of MBE scores from other jurisdictions. The examination is administered in February and July each year during the last week of the month that includes a Wednesday.

On Tuesday, applicants will have three hours during the morning session to answer three essay questions; during the afternoon session, applicants will have three hours and 30 minutes to answer two essay questions and one PT. Each essay question is designed to be answered in one hour and the PT is designed to be completed in 90 minutes. The MBE will be administered on Wednesday. Applicants with disabilities granted extended time accommodations will have slightly different schedules. Notwithstanding this change, everything in this book remains pertinent and applicable as an aid in earning a passing score under the current format.

Curtis L Howard Jr. Esq.

# ABOUT THE AUTHOR

"I came from a place where not following the rules was the rule. To be different, I followed the rules and achieved. Now I've learned, to be the best you have to think outside the box and that means sometimes not following the rules."

- Curtis L. Howard Jr.

Circa 1979 a hot summer day in south central Los Angeles provides the backdrop as a teenaged boy on his moped talks to a young girl who lives on his block. Attracted to her the boy asks for her phone number. Intrigued by his attention the girl proposes, "if you can guess the last four digits I'll give you the first three." Quick on his feet the boy guesses the last four digits of the number as the address of the house where she lived. This is how the relationship between my mother and father began which would ultimately lead to my being in this world.

My mother taught me to be, "different" from the other kids in my neighborhood. Why, I wondered. The other boys at school wore jeans, T-shirts and sneakers, while I wore cardigan sweaters and neck ties. I can recall her referring to me as studious. That is how she wanted me to be. Then I received a phone call that would change my life. "Aye Curt, somebody just hit Tom in the head with a bottle and they robbing his liquor store!" I immediately thought about walking past Tom's Liquor on my way home from Raymond Avenue elementary school that day. I couldn't believe the store was being was being robbed. Later in the day while watching the evening news with my grandmother, I discovered that my friend was mistaken. Tom's wasn't being robbed, it was being looted! At the intersection of Florence and Normandie the looters and loiterers had beaten Reginald Denny and Fidel Lopez as retaliation for the L.A.P. D's acquittal of assault and use of excessive force against Rodney King. What followed would be five days of pure mutiny. Stores were looted while arsonists set fires among rampant gunfire. Eventually the Los Angeles police department outfitted in full riot gear would attempt to quell the revolt, however, with hundreds of protestors flooding the streets the police were called off leading to an explosion of lawlessness and debauchery. In all, there were over 58 fatalities and the city would suffer millions of dollars in property damage.

My mother understood what it meant to attend school in that environment, therefore, she made the decision to have me bussed to Parkman Jr. High in Woodland Hills. I also attended Taft High School in the same district. Ventura Boulevard's sprawling upper middle-class landscape was a stark contrast to South Central. The cultural and visual disparity between the two communities caused me to think and then to ask why?

My colleague and dear friend Larry Webb speaks of what he calls, "The Why Doctrine." The doctrine states, "to begin the process of solving a particular challenge one must start each journey with a simple but profound question. Why? From my perspective, the point of this doctrine, is to ask, "why" as an exercise to develop the habit of questioning everything while on the path toward achieving one's goal. This is not a hard and fast answer as to why a set of circumstances occurred, but as a way of delving deeper into the path of personal growth.

I ask myself why is it necessary for me write this book? I wrote this book to share with you my story, my lessons and my pain with the hope that it will help you through your trial. I wrote this book as a cast off to a new journey as a licensed professional. This book marks a corner-stone in my crusade to give direction to those who need a guide. I hope that you also, begin to ask why more often and habitually question the cause and meaning of the circumstances that unfold as you strive for success. Lastly, this book is a tangible example of how a perceived negative can be transposed into something positive that can help others and be a profitable creative outlet! I'm excited and I hope that you are too so let's get started.

# HOW TO USE THIS BOOK

Read this book a week or two before you start your course study. Think of it as a primer to your exam course or self-study itinerary. Another Round at the Bar was written intentionally for the person gearing up for a tedious study regimen, meaning it's a relatively quick and easy read. I will not bog you down with burdensome tasks and assignments that add to your study anxiety.

When reading do not get caught up in over analyzing the material, just read it and take it for what it is. As you read ask yourself questions about the content, then mentally come up with short simple answers or opinions and move on. There are a few mental exercises that I suggest you participate in. They are there for your benefit, not to add to any compulsions you may have about doing everything in every book you read. They should only take a few minutes at the most to complete and most, if not all, are mental and do not require any writing. Most importantly don't fret if you do not complete them all or if you fail to practice them religiously. Again, they are there for your benefit not to give your more, "stuff" to do to pass your entrance exam. In, short HAVE FUN WITH IT!

After you have read this supplement cover to cover, keep it handy. Inside are tips and tricks for the day of your exam, quotable quotes and anecdotes that are great for keeping your spirits up during burnout periods. So, when you feel like just giving up (it happens to the best of us) pick up the book, go a section that resonated with you and be amazed how reading a few encouraging words can keep you going. Maybe you are feeling lost and alone during a period of lengthy study. Review some of the stories in the text (highlight them during your first read), reread them for reassurance that you are not alone and that others have experienced what you have and were ultimately successful. Also, right before your practice exams and the final exam, pick this book up and review the section on tips and tricks for exam day. Doing so will refresh your recollection on what pitfalls to look for and caveats that can help you avoid common mistakes.

Share share share! Undoubtedly you know someone in your situation (a repeat taker) so whenever you come across a chapter, section, exercise or idea you find helpful share it with a friend. Not only will it help the other person but sharing helps to ingrain that idea into your own mind making your test taking abilities that much stronger.

# ANOTHER ROUND AT THE BAR

By Curtis L. Howard Jr. Esq

# Clean Slate

Before you dive head first into the ocean of substantive data, practice multiple choice questions, essays and performance tests, you must first develop the proper mindset or perspective for preparing for your licensing exam. For example, getting ready for the California State Bar exam is a marathon, not a sprint, so you must prepare your mind for the psychological rollercoaster that comes with experiencing high highs and very low lows.

A quote from Werner Erhard, 1970s self-help guru sets the stage nicely for our first initiation. "Just because you perceive it doesn't mean it's real." We all have opinions about our abilities regarding the skills associated with taking and ultimately passing licensing exams: intelligence, punctuality and discipline, to name a few. Our attitude about these subjects comes from our parents, friends, colleagues, the media. Most importantly, it comes from the grades we earn on our tests. But from now on, we are going to change our negative perceptions considering Erhard's wisdom. Say this aloud, "my negative perceptions are not real." Again, "my negative perceptions are not real." Now pause and meditate on that idea. Try your hardest to believe what you are telling yourself. Clear out all negative thoughts, assumptions and beliefs you have regarding your professional school experience and previous attempts at licensing exams.

You may be saying to yourself, "If it's not real then why bother with it?" Let me explain. Your negative perception is real in the sense that it exists, but it is not real because it is not fact. You are in control of your attitude toward yourself and anything else, thus it can be changed. The key is to allow the positive aspects of an experience to dominate your vision while permitting the short-comings to act as signals alerting you to areas that require your attention.

As an example, I earned my J.D (Juris Doctor) from the New College School of Law. A small non-ABA accredited private law school in San Francisco California whose moniker was the, "oldest public interest" law school in California. Unfortunately, the school was acquired by another institution during my third and final year, so it no longer exists. During the school's acquisition, there were many hardships. Some of the faculty resigned from their positions, many under-classmen had to transfer to other schools, some students could not endure the transition and did not graduate.

Overall it was a discouraging and sometimes frightening experience. I questioned the post-graduate support and the stigma associated with

4

graduating from a law school that had "closed down." I could have allowed these facts to shape my perception of the New College. Instead I chose to focus on the meaning behind what the New College stood for. It provided an alternative to the traditional law school paradigm. At New College, we welcomed community, cooperation, diversity and a focus on how the law could be used in the public's interest. This environment was ideal for a unique brand of peer comradery that extended beyond competitiveness. Some of us have ventured into business together while others remain good friends outside of the law. The lesson is that The New College shaped my sense of how to marshal the law and that reflects on how I treat my clients.

Thinking of my law school experience in this light makes me extremely proud to be a member of the last class of the New College School of Law. Because the school has been acquired its brand of lawyering has become a rarity and I use this fact as a selling point to many of my clients who have had unfavorable experiences with more financially motivated lawyers. Not to say that I work solely pro bono, I do not. I do, however, present the most affordable approach to solving my client's legal issues and I got that sense from the New College. It would have been a lot easier for me to just accept the fact that my school was acquired and perceive it as something negative. I could have carried it around as a handy excuse for many hardships I faced during my Bar preparation and as a newly licensed attorney. But we do not have to do that, we have the power to change any perceived negative into a positive by focusing on the advantages any given circumstance offers.

I'm sure you have heard the old cliché about Robert F. Kennedy Jr. taking the Bar three times before he passed. But did you know that several other legal scholars and highly important government officials are also repeat takers? former First lady Michelle Obama, California Governor Jerry Brown, former Secretary of State Hillary Clinton and former U.S Supreme Court Justice Cardozo just to name a few. Yes, I said it, you can become a U.S Supreme Court Justice having taken the Bar more than once. Can you imagine the consequences of these admired and renowned public figures giving up on themselves after not passing the first time? Well they certainly would not be who and where they are today.

So, right here and now, give yourself a clean slate. Why? Because most of us are too critical of ourselves. I've said it all to myself, "I didn't study hard enough, I should have done more practice exams, I should have been more diligent when I was in school." Well, it may come as a surprise, but I passed my exam despite all that criticism. And it is impossible to know what improvements will get you over the hump, so don't worry about it. Even the most confident exam-takers have self-doubts and lack substantive knowledge. Your job is to do your best and try your hardest to improve.

First, apologize to yourself for not putting forth the effort you could have when a challenge presented itself. For example, you could say, "I'm sorry for not giving 100% when I knew I could have given more than I did." Now, forgive yourself for all your academic shortcomings or any disabilities you feel are holding you back from giving your all on your next prep. Are you a terrible speller? Do you read more slowly than you think you should be reading? Did you earn a C minus in a core class or elective in grad school? If you answered yes to any of these questions then right now say, "**I forgive myself**." Take a few minutes if necessary to reflect and truly forgive yourself.

A good faith apology and your acceptance are the basis for the personal promise you are going to make. Here and now make a promise to yourself to continue to improve on your weaknesses and bolster your strengths. This is the first step in developing the mind-set necessary to prepare for your licensing exam. *I challenge you to repeat this exercise throughout your preparation* and ultimately make it a life-long habit. To heighten effectiveness, practice identifying negative thoughts you have about yourself and replacing them with positive mantras. The next time you find yourself struggling with a perceived weakness don't scold yourself. Simply realize that you have identified your inefficiency in this area, take the necessary steps to mitigate your ineptitude (practice/research) and conclude knowing that overtime you will improve and reach proficiency. This process will realign your perspective during your practice exams when you aren't getting the results you desire. Here, right now - **Try the exercise again**.

EXERCISE: Clean Slate

<u>Step 1</u>: Identify some aspect of your academic skill set you feel is a weakness.

<u>Step 2</u>: Verbally apologize and forgive yourself for this inadequacy.

<u>Step 3</u>: Replace the negative belief with a promise to improve.

<u>Step 4</u>: Visualize yourself practicing a task that improves your weakness and see yourself performing well.

Until I developed this mindset I considered myself a below average speller. My spelling wasn't egregious, but I've seen plenty of squiggly red lines underneath misspelled words in my time (Thanks MS Word!). Today, if I'm not sure how to spell a word I make a good faith attempt to write/type it correctly. If I misspell the word, I simply look the word up and write or type it out again. I try to identify why this word gave me trouble and create a rule to clear up my misunderstanding. Finally, I give myself a mental "pat on the back" for taking the time out to become a better speller. And overtime, my spelling improved.

Here is another personal, yet more intimate example. I've always thought of myself as a smart guy. Not to be ostentatious but throughout my academic career I could always manage to maintain a solid B average without much effort. Some may consider this ability an asset and I was one of those people, until a challenge came along that required me to step my game up.

We talked earlier about how I graduated from The New College School of Law and how the school was acquired during my last two years there. Well this transition had a detrimental effect on my academic performance. My first year I earned a respectable 3.0 G.P.A. I was satisfied with that average and planned to do as I usually did and do just enough work to maintain it. Looking back, I'm ashamed of setting such a low standard for myself, but it worked for me in the past and I saw no reason to push myself any harder than I had to (that was a mistake). Once the New College acquisition started to wind down, some of the professors resigned, classes were cancelled and a laissez faire attitude took over the campus. Before you point your finger and say I'm about to use this as an excuse for the drop in my G.P.A, I'll clarify.

I take full responsibility for my lack of focus and maturity during the New College acquisition. During my 2L and 3L years not only were my substantive classes less interesting to me (I had already taken criminal law, criminal procedure and evidence, the classes necessary for a criminal lawyer) but the classroom structure became increasingly unstable. Instead of buckling down, trying harder and seeking guidance, I just kept with my usual study habits. They were insufficient to maintain my 3.0 average. Granted, I never failed a class but my G.P.A suffered.

To this day, I still struggle with truly forgiving myself for how I responded when the situation called for more diligence. To cope, I remind myself that I'm not perfect. I know that so long as I continue to recognize my mistakes and don't repeat them, I'm doing my part towards furthering self-improvement. Take a message from my story in that you can overcome the burden of past indiscretions. Failure occurs only when we refuse to admit and remedy our mistakes. And never quit because a slip-up can be corrected.

If you are a person with issues regarding your self-worth or your academic prowess counseling may be an option. Counseling can be scheduled sessions with a paid professional psychologist or psychiatrist, a weekend self-help seminar or just a chat with a close friend. Don't be afraid to confide in someone who can give you another perspective about aspects of what you perceive to be personal failings. You may find that some of your friends and family think very highly of you and that they too lack of confidence. (remember the lyrics to the song, SING! you are not alone...) Although it is difficult to believe you will pass your exam if you have severe self-doubt, your preparation will be more productive once you have freed yourself from your personal insecurities. Easier said than done, yes. But it is necessary and absolutely worth your time.

Everyone in pursuit of a worthy goal faces multiple obstacles. Some are unavoidable, some are externally imposed and others we create for ourselves. It is our job to destroy those obstacles that we create. We must learn how to over-come all challenges, whether it be through finesse or brute-force. Self-loathing and doubt, however, are self-made and we must not allow them to prevent us from crossing the finish line. The following is an example of a family member who faced some common hurdles in her journey toward a successful and fulfilling life.

My aunt, Flora Pierce-Williams was a college graduate and general contractor who owned a thriving real estate brokerage in Los Angeles. She was a single mother of three boys who moved to L.A. from Ohio in the 1970's to pursue a career in real estate. As an African-American female general contractor she experienced sexism in construction, a male dominated profession. This obstacle could have been the demise of her aspirations, however, she never let those perceived disadvantages keep her from staying committed to her goal. Before her retirement, Flora owned her own real estate brokerage and multiple residential properties. She managed several multi-unit dwellings as well as brokered countless mortgages.

As a Toastmaster and conductor of seminars for young girls, her influence extends beyond real-estate and contracting. Throughout my life, she has been a constant source of valuable advice. Once as a young man in undergraduate school she advised, "Curtis, success depends largely on the people you know and the books you read." I'd like to add to her advice and stress that yes you must read, but you must also *PRACTICE* the tasks in the books you read. How many books have you read cover to cover only to neglect the propositions that call you to action? It's not as if you can read the caveats and exercises once and expect your mind-set to change. To put it frankly, the exercises in this book are not magic. They will only work if you read them, study them, and implement them with conviction. Like most things in life, you must practice the exercises for them to work! Practice means so much repetition that eventually the exercise becomes a habit. So much of a habit that you can perform these mental exercises sub-consciously without thinking or expending any noticeable energy. Does this mean that you should religiously do the clean slate exercise for every little doubt you have about yourself? NO! That would-be counter-productive. The best practice is a mix of conscious planned effort and informal impromptu practice when the moment strikes you.

For example, you may want to sit down after reviewing a practice exam and note an area where you are constantly having trouble. Then perform the clean slate exercise to avoid frustration. Or you may be walking in a shopping mall feeling upset about your exam, take a quick second to practice steps 3 and 4 of the clean slate exercise to reassure yourself that you are improving on your weaknesses then quickly visualize yourself practicing and getting better results.

Another way to help you learn to forgive yourself is to make a list of skills you do well and review the list regularly. Maybe you are proficient with punctuation and have a large vocabulary. Maybe you are a pretty good issue spotter or have a knack for memorizing rules. Keep a mental note of your list, and add new traits as you think of them. Be sure to write them down and carry them with you in a note pad or your phone. Over time, you may find that you're developing quite a sizeable list and, not coincidentally, a much more positive attitude about yourself. So, when you get discouraged (because you will) remind yourself of the skills you have mastered, and qualities others have complimented you on. This exercise will help you avoid frustration and negative thoughts that drain the energy required to review mistakes and make corrections.

For some of us, figuring out exactly why we have faults is a good way to overcome them. Here is a great exercise from a book called, *Study Skills for Science Students* by Daniel D. Chiras that helps with this process. First, take a piece of paper and divide it into four vertical columns. In column 1, list the traits, you don't like. In column 4, list how you would like to be. For example, if you're not an avid reader, you might want to be comfortable with reading more to improve your comprehension.

In column 2, list the reasons why you behave or feel the way you do now. Why are you not an avid reader? Were your parents' non-readers, were they the type to occupy you with the television? Did you need glasses as a child making it difficult for you to see and thus you avoided reading? For example, does it make sense to not read more just because you watched a lot of television as a child or because you don't fully comprehend everything you read on the first try?

After analyzing why, you are the way you are, list steps you'll take to change. Place these ideas in column 3. For example, you might begin by setting short, manageable goals for your next leisure reading, like five to ten pages. Allow yourself to stop reading once you have reached your goal and return when you are refreshed and ready to read again. Over time increase your goal as you get more comfortable reading more pages. Work your way up until you are reading whole chapters in one sitting.

Again, the point of the clean-slate and the other exercises in this book is not to bog you down with more stuff to do. The best way to do these exercises is once on paper and then get in the habit of performing them mentally when you feel frustrated or overwhelmed. Remember that your perception of your ability directly affects how you will prepare and ultimately perform.

You cannot expect to do your best on your licensing exam if you do not believe that your best is good enough. Moreover, do not allow what may easily be classified as a disadvantage to veer you off your course of action. Take a few moments to identify some aspects of yourself, life experiences or academic career that may appear to be disadvantages. Then take a second glance and look at them from an alternative prospective and find a way to see them as assets.

# Making an Honest Self-Assessment

Now that you are a forgiving mood you must do an honest assessment of your previous study schedule and the effort you put out to see it through. Some of us assume that all we need to do is brush up on a subject or get just a few more points in each section. But, if you are on your third, fourth or fifth attempt then your problem is not just lack of substantive knowledge it is more likely a fundamental flaw in your preparation.

You cannot make an accurate assessment if you cannot be honest with yourself. Keep in mind that you have already forgiven yourself for your imperfections and are committed to improving. Remember an honest assessment is part of improving. Now, go find your study schedule from your last prep, let's analyze it.

What do you have in front you? If you have never used a formal written study schedule don't panic or feel ashamed we will discuss that later. For those of you who have created your own study schedules I'd like you to breakdown the format you used. Did you organize by subject? For example, subject 1 week 1 then subject 2 the next week etc. Or did you break it up by test section? Multiple choice week 1, essays week two, performance tests week 3 and so on?  No matter how detailed and thorough your schematic may appear it is likely lacking in one key area, "institutional memory."

Understand that the test you are preparing for is part of an institution.  In some cases, the test itself is its own entity aside from the graduate school experience. Whether it be law, medicine, real-estate or plumbing there is a history associated with the "final exam" used to determine whether you are ready to practice.  The committees who create these tests are well-versed in said history and expect a very particular answer to the questions they have meticulously drafted. What is institutional memory?   I define the term as an institution's course of preparation that covers commonly tested subject matter designed to achieve competence.  Institutional memory can only be developed through years of experience and trial and error.

Do not make it your goal to create the perfect study schedule through trial and error.  There are others whose profession it is to figure out exactly what the test creators want and how to prepare you to provide them the answers they want.  Your job is to have faith in a prep-course and give a one-hundred percent effort.  Their job is to provide you with the tools to pass if you put forth a sustained high-level effort.  Just do your job and let them do their job.  Yes, the fee for their service is not cheap and many people reasonably feel uncomfortable paying for a prep-course right after paying tuition for graduate school. I can recall saying before my first attempt at the California State Bar, "I refuse to pay any more money to prepare for a test that law school should have prepared me for!" Little did I know my attitude put me on a course for the long haul.

Licensing exams can take on a life of their own and can seem daunting after all the time and money already spent on your professional education. I am not suggesting that you cannot pass without taking a professional course, you can, and many have in the past and will in the future. Nor am I saying that your education is not necessary to pass your exam, it is! What I am suggesting is that there is a level of practice, knowledge of testable subject matter and test specific nuances that are only taught in professional prep-courses. Many of us get close to passing and understand the general concepts being tested, however, it is the *fine line details* that keep us from getting over the hump.

Undoubtedly, no matter what I say there will be people who have convinced themselves that they cannot afford a professional prep-course (that was my excuse for several attempts). Others will simply be unable to cope with the fact that they must pay more money and take yet another class just to pass their licensing exam. If you refuse to pay for a professional course, then you must create your own study schedule.  I would search for study schedules through used professional prep course materials or peers who have taken your exam and integrate some of their concepts into your own. For example, I created a variety of my own study regimens before I finally passed.

One key task missing from the plans I created and the one that ultimately lead to a passing effort was *taking a full practice exam just a few days before the actual exam.*  What can you think of that is missing from your schedule?

For those who have taken prep classes that provided full schedules I'd suggest you reinvest your faith in the company you paid and rely on their expertise in creating a proper schedule. Certainly, you may want to tailor it to fit your individual needs but in general you should follow their guidelines.  Decisions concerning the order in which you study subjects or how many essays to write or how many multiple-choice questions you should do, are best deferred to the professionals who create prep-course study schedules.

Then there are those of us who don't have any kind of study schedule.  Don't worry, I didn't forget about you.  A schedule doesn't work for you because you're busy with family and work. Or maybe you aren't good at creating or keeping schedules. Maybe you are a person who is a whiz at memorizing things and works best adjusting on the fly. To quote preparatory professional Bob Hull, "that's all to the good" but unfortunately, you probably won't pass until you understand that the preparation for your licensing exam must follow a pre-determined study schedule.

How you integrate the schedule into your life is a personal challenge, but the fact is *you must have a consistent practice regimen that is proven to improve the analytical skills necessary to pass your exam*. The established prep courses have years of test related knowledge and experience (institutional memory) that is factored into the creation of their study schedules. Their pass/fail statistics tell them what works and what doesn't. This institutional memory enables them to weed out unnecessary subject matter and busy work. If you don't have a study schedule get one from a prep course, borrow one from a colleague or make your own. Point is - you must have one.

EXERCISE TWO: Study Schedule Critique

With schedule in hand, give it a big picture review. Review the following questions and reflect on your answers. Then improve your current study schedule with additions related to your answers.

1. Did you make notes?  What do they say?
2. Overall were the assignments realistically achievable considering your available study time?
3. Any exercises or practice drills missing?
4. Did your schedule's difficulty increase as your test date approached?
5. How much time was allocated to substantive review vs. actual practice?
6. How much time was allocated for rest?
7. Did you allot time to practice under *time pressure*?
8. Does your schedule call for a full practice exam?
9. Was there a plan to take a full practice test day before the actual exam?

### SEEING THE SCHEDULE THROUGH

With an improved schedule, you can now turn your attention to the commitment required to complete all your assignments and see your schedule all the way through.  Werner Erhard said it best, "have a commitment to producing a result, then looking back to see what it took to produce that result."  Here, the result you are committed to produce is a level of preparedness sufficient to pass your licensing exam.

When I consider the range of effort I put out on my five attempts at the California State Bar there was clearly a gradual increase of effort from first to last. The first time I took the California State Bar I was arrogant and naïve. I did not research any prep courses or information regarding what it took to pass the exam. I foolishly figured that since I passed my law school exams, I could review a few outlines, do some multiple-choice questions and practice essays and I would pass. I was wrong!

On my first attempt, I figured a full review of substantive law was in order. For the first few months I sat at home and in the library reading outlines like one would read a fiction novel. For some subjects, I would even re-write what was already in the outline. Yes, I was outlining the outlines! This did me absolutely no good. When I finally started to practice essays and multiple-choice questions I found myself unable to cite the rules of law because I hadn't memorized them. As a result, during and after my practice questions I'd find myself back in the outlines looking for the rules of law that I'd read and sometimes outlined weeks ago.

Finally, the day of my exam came and despite being ill-prepared I came close to passing the first time. This fact created a false sense of security. After a review of my scores, I figured if I get a few more points here and a few more points there, I'd pass on my second attempt.

Here is where it starts to get tricky. On my second attempt, I wised up and paid for a course. However, I'd convinced myself that I could not afford a traditional course, so I paid for a private course at a reduced cost. I started the course full of energy, but I had the mentality that all I was there to do was, "brush up" on the areas I'd scored low on during my first attempt. My attitude resulted in a half-hearted attempt that left me ill-prepared to get the points I needed to pass.

For example, when I was assigned tasks covering subjects I felt I already knew I would write what I thought were passing papers. I would get my assignments back full of red lines and corrections and I'd become furious. I can recall thinking that the grader was being too critical of my answers because I knew that I had done a sufficient job and he/she was just nitpicking. I was wrong. The grader was pointing out that I was not answering the question in a way the Bar graders wanted. For the first time, I was faced with the reality that I didn't know the Bar standard. My answers consistently came up a little short, whether it was because of incorrect format, readability, missing issues or deficient analysis. Instead of humbling myself and seeing the direction for what it was I remained arrogant and concluded that the graders were just being pretentious.  Besides I'd come close to passing the first time and I was just there to brush up on a few subjects.

Because of my attitude, I failed to complete all the assignments.  The instructor stressed the importance of creating a schedule, but I did not follow through.  No surprise, I did not pass the second time and even lost a few points here and there. I basically got the same score as I did the first time.  It was then that I'd arrived in Egypt for my spring vacation because I was in denial.

I told myself, "it was not my fault I didn't pass."  I had an air-tight list of excuses:  I paid for a private course, they didn't give me a schedule, they didn't give me a set of new shiny outlines and a huge book of multiple choice questions, etc.  Sadly, at that time I did not understand that I had not put forth the effort necessary to give the course a chance to work.  I had not yet humbled myself to the point where I knew I had to work toward competence.

What's the old cliché, third times the charm?  Well here we go!  On the third attempt, I'd reviewed my scores and realized that, "all I needed to do" was improve on the essay section and I would pass.  Yes, this is it.  Numbers never lie.  Just a few higher scores on my essays then I would be over the top, besides the essays counted for the highest percentage of possible points.  My plan was to do enough essays per subject so that I would cover nearly every possible testable scenario. Genius! Emboldened, I set off to do 88 Bar essays from the Bar website and the used prep-books I'd accumulated.

There was no lack of effort on my third attempt, I'd charted 11 subjects and set out to do eight essays per subject. I created a spreadsheet and placed it on my wall so that after completing each essay I would put the date and time I completed it to hold myself accountable. There was no way I wouldn't ace every essay. One problem though, I didn't have a grader!

To compensate for the lack of a grader I compared my essays to the model answers found in books or web-sites. In hind's sight, it was like the dumb leading the ignorant. I was like gang-busters grading the first 30 essays. I meticulously combed through each paragraph doing line by line comparisons between what I wrote and what the model answer told me what the, "right answer" was. Then fatigue set in and by essay number fifty, not only did I lessen the scrutiny with which I was grading, I had somehow mysteriously began writing perfect essays. What I mean by that is the model answer analyses began to be inaccurate in my opinion and they were misquoting the law, so I thought how could this be the, "right" answer? Some were missing issues and forgetting to analyze key exceptions. By this time, I knew my answers were clearly better. This is the type of delusion you develop when you are on your third attempt of the California State Bar and cabin fever has started to set in.

I took the Bar for the third time and earned nearly the same score as my first two attempts. This taught me that a bull-rush of preparation on one section will not lead to a passing effort, even if the chosen section makes up the largest percentage of points.

Ah, what to do, what to? I was losing my motivation, energy and the will to keep trying. I'd depleted my financial resources paying for the three previous Bar attempts and didn't know where more money to take it again would come from. Honestly, I just wanted to find a job doing anything so I could forget I ever went to law school.

Then suddenly out of the blue, I got a call from my aunt Cheryl Williams. I hadn't spoken to her in over ten years! She knew that I graduated from law school, so I explained that I had yet to pass the Bar and was unsure of how I would pay for another attempt. After all I'd endured, I knew that I needed to pay for a full professional course so I told her that I needed close to 4,000 dollars for the course and test.

She understood my struggle and initiated a donation campaign and raised over seven-hundred dollars for me to take the Bar again. It was not enough to pay for a course, however, I was extremely grateful that someone appreciated all the effort I'd put into becoming a Bar applicant and sacrificed their own money, time and energy to give me another shot.

Since I did not have the funds to pay for a course I set out to prepare evenly for all three sections of the Bar. I factored all the lessons I'd learned from my previous three attempts into a comprehensive study schedule. I learned from my first attempt to keep outlining and substantive review to a reasonable minimum. From my second attempt, I learned to give a one-hundred percent effort and dismiss the, "brush up" attitude. From my third attempt, I learned that doing an avalanche of essays without a grader would not improve my scores in that section. These were time consuming and expensive lessons to learn but I was determined not to repeat those mistakes on my fourth try.

I can remember sitting on a bench in the playground of the apartment complex I lived in at the time. This is where I watched my kids play and practiced my daily quota of multiple choice questions. At the time, I was a stay at home dad so I spent a lot of time in the house watching the kids. Since I rarely got a chance to get out of the house, on days like this I appreciated the sun on my back and the cool breeze brushing my shoulders while I pondered why choice A was a "better" choice than C. The trials of the years past created an attitude of gratefulness for the mere opportunity to take the Bar so I made it a point to *enjoy my study time.*

My fourth attempt was more about learning how to integrate studying into my daily routine rather than treating it as something separate from my family life. This time around my mantra would be to, "rest to avoid burnout and frustration." I remembered my previous attempts worrying about every detail and overworking myself and that did not make for better scores. On this fourth time, I followed the schedule I created. I rested when I got tired. And when I got a question incorrect I did not get upset, instead I tried to understand why (remember the why doctrine) the examiners preferred their answer over mine (most of the time their answers were rooted in a more thorough analysis).

I didn't pass on my fourth attempt, but I was at peace with it. A review of my scores revealed a significant increase on the multiple-choice section but my essays and performance tests scores remained subpar. It was a bitter-sweet time. I failed the test again, but on the bright side I was now privy to something more valuable than passing, I'd discovered the preparation necessary to reach the Bar standard (at least the multiple-choice section). I figured that so long as I applied the same preparation that I did for the multiple choice to all three sections I would pass. I was mentally ready for my fifth and final bout with the Bar.

Before I go into my last prep story allow me to digress. Much of what I learned from the first four attempts had to do *with me*, not the Bar. By that I mean my attitude, my views about life and my appreciation for opportunity were all changed for the better. Looking back, it was never a question of intelligence that kept me from passing it was an issue of maturity. We all have insecurities and immature habits that keep us from realizing our full potential. And sometimes we are not allowed to transition to our next phase until we get it right.

I remember telling my aunt Cheryl that I did not pass. She seemed a little disappointed, but I was confident that I was ready to pass next time. For my fifth and final try I knew I needed to pay for another course, so I researched all the standard Bar review courses. By this time, my wife was making decent money, so we made the decision to use our entire tax refund to finance my fifth attempt.

I paid extra money to do an, "early bird" course to eliminate any excuses for being unprepared. This course started nearly six months before the Bar with close to two months of pure substantive review followed by in class study sessions. It was then I made a promise to myself to put it all on the line, leave nothing left on the table (insert your favorite cliché) and *complete each-and-every task assigned.* The course provided a pre-determined work/study schedule, essay graders and a full mock Bar just days before the actual Bar. I know what you are thinking, and yes, I did say you should limit your substantive review, but this course taught the black letter law in a way that I'd never considered.

One day while in class Bob Hull, the instructor for my course, and I were talking about my last four attempts. I told him about how I poured hours and hours into substantive review but never really retained any of it. He inquired how I went about my review and I told him I would listen to audio mp3s and read outlines then outline the outlines. After my response, I expected Bob to look puzzled, but he did not look surprised. He told me others in the past had made that same mistake. He said taking the Bar that way is like taking the test with only half of your brain. He explained that this course would teach me the substantive law through creating and using *flow charts.* First, I would fill in the flow chart while watching lectures on the internet then use the flow charts during my practice exams. Bob also said that once it came time to recall rules and issues during the Bar my brain would have a visual aid to help me remember what I needed.

Now some of you reading this may think, "that's obvious, everyone knows that visual cues are the best tools for recalling information." Funny thing is I was somewhat aware of the value of flow charts but never consistently used them during law school. As a result, when it came time to prepare for the Bar, the flow chart method was not a part of my preparation.

Moreover, the course created flow charts using its institutional memory to narrow down the testable issues and eliminate unnecessary elements, my job was just to fill in the definitions. Had I created my own flowcharts they would have undoubtedly been far too detailed limiting their practicability. Lesson being is that even if you are aware of a successful preparation method it may still have to be presented to you in a way that is best suited for the test you are preparing for. Maybe a person of authority or whom you hold in high regard may have to suggest it to you before you give it true consideration. The key is to find a way to revive old problem-solving methods you may have overlooked in the past. Then give them a rehash, use them more often and in varying contexts, you may find that tools you have previously ignored, or cast-off are an untapped resource.

For two months, I sat in my office, listing to video lectures and filling in flow charts. I was so diligent Bob once responded in an e-mail that I was ahead (preparation wise) of 99% of people gearing up for the next Bar. With the wind under my sails I was ready to start the in-class sessions.

When class started, I was full of energy but knew from past experiences that I was not there to raise my hand at every chance to try and prove to myself and everyone that I had studied. Instead I participated when I felt it was necessary, and asked questions only after I tried to answer the question myself first. Unlike my first course, this time I did not become combative when I received my graded essays. I simply rewrote them with the graders suggestions in mind and understood that I would always miss some issue or element and lived with it. I made it a priority to do multiple choice questions from a variety of sources including those in books I'd come across in past attempts.

I can recall a conversation with Bob where I told him that I was learning so much from the class. I felt some discomfort from this statement because I'd taken this test four times and there was still so much I didn't know. Then Bob explained how he'd taken the Bar far more times than I as part of being an instructor and that he still learns something new or discovers a novel analysis for the same issues he'd seen time and time again. Here, I really started to understand that passing the Bar was about competence not mastery.

As the final weeks of the course approached the schedule's difficulty increased. However, I stuck to my promise and completed every assignment. Eventually the time came for us to self-administer a full mock Bar a few days before the actual Bar. I did so and even after all the studying I still didn't score off the charts. I scored right in the passing range. There I was, at the end of the prep road and let me tell you I was not 100 percent sure I'd pass. But I'd come this far not for that purpose, but for another one entirely. I'd gone through all four previous attempts to come to the point where I could be confident that I gave a 100 percent effort and did everything in my power to prepare for my next challenge, and essentially, I had already passed the real test!

During my previous attempts, I'd always run into a familiar face at the test site. Sometimes I would see an old law school classmate. On another occasion, I was reacquainted with an old friend from undergraduate school. But this time, there was no one. I took the Bar all alone so to speak and a melancholy feeling came over me. I felt like the last of my class who would try and crack this thing, but I was also proud of my perseverance.

On this attempt the essay questions seemed easier than the practice questions I'd taken for the class. I finished the multiple-choice section early and my performance tests were much more organized and written in the proper format. The effort I put out toward this class had prepared me so well that one question felt like a plug and play computer part. Let me explain. I could hear Bob's voice as I visualized the flow chart outlining the legal analysis for a civil procedure question in front of me. The hypothetical was short and to the point purposefully leaving plenty of room for conjecture.

Sometimes the Bar examiners try and lure examinees into second guessing their analysis by leaving room to argue superfluous elements and/or irrelevant facts. Their goal is to test your time management skills. I was not fooled by their ruse, I simply stuck to the elements contained in the flow chart and dispensed with the one-hour question in 30 minutes.

When the Bar was over I took the train home not expecting anything special, but to my surprise my wife and kids baked me a chocolate cake with the words, "We're so proud of you" written in blue icing. That was a great moment of validation. I had done all I could and no matter the outcome my family recognized my effort without any self-proclamation.

Fast forward nearly four months. I received a letter from the Bar in the mail. I took it to my office where my oldest daughter sat. I opened the envelope and I'll never forget reading those words, "The Committee of Bar Examiners of the State Bar of California is delighted to report that you achieved a passing score on the July 2012 administration of the California Bar Examination. Congratulations; you may justly be proud of your achievement." I immediately picked my daughter up and hugged her tightly and said, "I passed, I passed the Bar." She seemed happier about it than I was. Looking back, it was all worth it.

The point of reiterating my past Bar attempts was so that you can *learn from my mistakes* as well as get a sense of where you can improve in your preparation. Were you able to recognize some of your own bad habits in my story? Maybe yes, maybe no. The point is to get you to think about your previous attempts critically. Not in a superficial sense, for example, I need to study subject A or B more. But on a deeper, more intimate level that addresses your level of effort and the method with which you chose to prepare. Considering my story and with your own efforts in mind, it is time for you to go through the process of discernment. What's required is an unemotional evaluation of your effort. To start, try this exercise.

EXERCISE THREE:  Work Ethic Critique

Think back to the first time you prepared for your exam and answer these questions honestly.

Try to be as objective as possible not being too hard on yourself but also being realistic and sincere.

1. Did you complete all assigned tasks?
2. Did you feel like your preparation tested your comfort zones?
3. Did you rest when you got fatigued or frustrated?
4. Did you take significant time off for any reason, excusable or not?
5. Did you start strong but your effort waned overtime?
6. Can you honestly say that you gave a one-hundred percent effort?

Now that you have looked back at the first time you studied for your exam, recall each subsequent attempt and repeat the process until you get to the last one. Do you recognize any patterns? What productive things do you do that produce positive results? Are there goals you fail to reach each time? What tasks are missing from each attempt? After answering these questions and others that you can think of take some time, a day or two to mull over what you have learned from reviewing your past study schedules and the effort you put out to complete them.

Remember not to be too hard on yourself, we are all human, we all make mistakes and the road to success is a process filled with some striking victories but mostly picking yourself up after a hard fall. If need be, re-visit the clean slate exercise and once again forgive yourself for the shortcomings you have discovered. The point is to internalize what you have learned about your past efforts. If you have the energy write some of those bad habits and pesky patterns down, this paper can act as an insurance policy to protect you from repeating them on your next attempt.

# Reassessing Your Exam

"If David had closed his eyes because he was too afraid of Goliath's size, he wouldn't have known how high to aim his sling."

-   Curtis L. Howard Jr.

Our next chapter concerns an emotion that we have all experienced, fear. Sometimes we subconsciously avoid looking our enemy right in the eye because we are unsure we will be able to defeat him. Prior to my first attempt I never researched the California State Bar's overall pass/fail statistics in depth. I'm not positively certain why I didn't look it up. Despite all the rumors I heard from classmates about the Bar being a difficult test, I was comfortable assuming that most students passed and only the bottom 20 or 30 percent had to retake the exam. After taking the exam for the first time I soon discovered that the California State Bar had approximately a 50 percent pass rate for July and about a 35 percent pass rate for February. Had I been more cognizant of these statistics early on maybe I would have had a better understanding of what it means to compete against hundreds of applicants all trying to do their best under time pressure. My advice to you, familiarize yourself with your test's statistical pass-fail rate and memorize its overall format.

Generally, you can find all sorts of statistical data for your exam on the web. For example, say you are taking the medical college admissions test? Simply type MCAT into Google, Bing or any other search engine and look for the official website for that exam (the official site is usually hosted by the administering committee). The site will usually have a tab or link containing current data for its overall passing score, what score range warrants a second read, what are passing scores for each individual section, understanding how scores are calculated, pass/fail rates and percentages by administration, demographical breakdowns of scores by schools or regions and even procedures for having your exam rescored. Also, browse the site thoroughly. Look for links and tabs that may be of some use to you. For example, the California Department of Real Estate website www.dre.ca.gov has an advice for examinees tab which contains useful do's and don'ts for exam applicants.

When dealing with statistics regarding your exam your goal is to get an overall general sense of how applicants fair on any given administration. Caveat, don't rely too much on these numbers as an indication of your chances of passing. For example, if you notice that the July Bar has a higher pass rate don't forgo taking it in

February just because you think you have a better chance in July. Of course, a higher pass rate may be one factor to consider but it should not be the sole determining fact. Also, if you notice significant discrepancies either between scores or pass/fail rates for different administrations of your exam don't spend any time attempting to figure out why these variances exist (an exception to the why doctrine). Simply make a mental note and give it some consideration when deciding when to take your exam. Remember, your goal as a repeat taker is to identify and remedy the shortcomings you have in your preparation for your exam not to find shortcuts. Relying on the fact that you have spent time and energy exploiting favorable statistics will not provide you with the tools necessary to pass your exam or to overcome adversity in your future career as a professional.

## EXERCISE FOUR:  Knowing Test Statistics

Here are a few questions regarding statistical data, you should review the answers to these questions and others that you can think of. Remember statistical data should be used only as factors in making test taking decisions - not as the sole basis. The answers to these questions can give you a better sense of where and when taking your exam will be most advantageous for you.

1. What is the pass/fail rate for your exam?
2. Does that rate differ by location or date of administration?
3. What is a passing overall score for your exam?
4. What is a passing score for each individual section?
5. Does your test offer a second read? If so what score mandates a second read?
6. How many people take the exam per administration?
7. Does the number of people taking the exam differ by location or date of administration?

## ADMINISTRATIVE REQUIREMENTS AND MACRO FORMAT

Now that you have a general sense of the statistics associated with your exam familiarize yourself with its administrative requirements and macro format. By administrative requirements I mean what you can and cannot do or bring or fail to bring to the test. By macro format I mean a general overview regarding which subjects your exam tests, time restraints, number of sections, number of questions per section and how much time should be allotted to each question.

Before you are let into the testing site many examinations have restrictions and requirements concerning whether you will be allowed to sit for the exam. A subtle but important oversight can possibly cost you hours in exam time, a full day or even a forfeiture of the entire administration if your exam is only a few hours long. I will use the California State Bar to illustrate this example, but you can apply the same principles to your exam.

Let's start with what you must bring to the exam. The California State Bar requires the applicant to bring his/her valid identification and their exam enrollment slip. For those taking the Bar on a computer you must bring your own, as computers will not be provided. Be aware that although not required, applicants can bring to the test on assigned days supplies like pencils, erasers, pillows, ear plugs and analogue clocks. Be aware that these allowances may have restrictions attached to them like limitations on quantity, type or how they are contained (inside a clear plastic baggy). These allowances and restrictions may change without notice at any time, so for a complete and current list please check with the committee of examiners and *do not* solely rely on what I've suggested here.

You must know yourself and try to imagine any necessity or discomfort you may encounter during your test and prepare for it. Are you the type of person who needs water often? If yes, know ahead of time if you can bring water bottles into the testing site, otherwise you may have to sacrifice test time to go to the water fountain.  Do your legs and/or butt get cramped easily from sitting for long periods?  If yes, research ahead of time if you can bring seat cushions and any restrictions on dimensions.  Usually multiple-choice sections require a number two pencil, make sure to bring plenty.  You don't want to be the person walking around minutes before the test asking people if you can borrow a pencil.  Just imagine being the person whose one pencil breaks during the exam and is forced to ask the proctor if they have one.  What if the proctor doesn't have one or there's a policy that forbids them from giving one to you.  In this situation you have lost time, added to your anxiety and possibly forfeited the remainder of your exam all due to a small oversight.

I can recall taking the Bar and being sanctioned for bringing something in that was not allowed.  I had a digital clock.  I'd used a digital clock during my preparation so that's what I was comfortable with.  I brought the clock in, sat it on my desk and took the first portion of the exam.  After the section was over one of the proctors approached my table. I promptly received a lecture about the importance of following the rules and was told to remove the clock from the testing area.  Although my sanction was mild.  (Being told to remove the clock from my table) I suffered greatly.  Firstly, having to overcome the emotion associated with being told I couldn't have my clock and secondly, adjusting my test strategy to take the test without a clock added to my anxiety. Trust me when you have prepared months in advance for a test, even the smallest mishaps can push you into a severe panic, so it's best to be prepared.

But don't get worked up trying to ensure you have covered all your bases. Why? Because even when fully prepared something always goes awry. The point is, take some time to think about the kind of accommodations you will need to be comfortable. Also consider what tools may be necessary for you to complete your exam to the best of your ability, then, research what the administrative requirements and restrictions are and prepare accordingly. A good way to prepare is with a checklist. The night or morning before your test, go through your checklist and make sure you have everything you need. You don't want to sacrifice time or bomb a section because you forgot to bring the power cord to your computer or not be allowed to sit for the exam because you don't have your identification. Trust me it has happened to some people. Can you think of any other administrative requirements not mentioned here?

## Macro View

An excellent place to start your macro view is knowing verbatim which subjects can be tested on your exam. When I took the California State Bar there were approximately fourteen testable subjects (depending on how you categorized them) including California specific law for evidence and civil procedure. The MBE or multiple-choice section is clear on which subjects will be tested and the performance test has all the law supplied in the library, so there is no ambiguity with these sections. However, there is a shroud of mystery and secrecy around which subjects will appear on the essay portions of the exam. Do not spend any time trying to figure out which subjects are going to be tested on the essay portions. Why? Firstly, you would be spending valuable time on something that will likely not be of any use. Secondly, I'm sure there is some method to how the examiners choose the subjects that appear on the essay portion, however, outside of the committee no one knows what that method is. The subjects may be randomly selected or chosen by algorithm. The point is don't waste your time trying to predict which subjects will appear on the essay only to foolishly base your study schedule according to those predictions.

Some preparatory courses provide students with their own predictions based on their institutional memory. Even such gifts are presented with a caveat for students to not solely rely on their predictions. It is said that some students who mistakenly do so receive a heightened understanding of the phrase "detrimental reliance." For tests that include multiple subjects some of which are tested while others may not be, the applicant should give each testable subject equal consideration. Of course, the student must consider which subjects they feel more comfortable with versus those she knows are troublesome. Here, subjects that cause you more difficulty should be given more attention while subjects that you are competent in or have mastered may receive less. Point being, predictions and difficultly are factors that help determine how to allocate study time between all testable subjects. *Do not forgo preparing for a subject based on predictions or because you feel you have mastered it.*

Next, let's turn our attention to how much time you have to complete your test. A California State Bar examinee for the general Bar has exactly twelve and a half hours divided into two days at six and a half hours the first day and six hours the second day. Day, one has, three, one-hour essays then a one-hour break. After the break, the examinee answers two additional one-hour essays and one 90-minute performance test. Day two is made up of the MBE, three hours for the first section, then a one-hour break. Then three hours for the last section. Exact start, break and end times are determined by the committee of Bar examiners. I'd like for you to research this information for your test. How long do you have to take your exam and exactly how do the examiners divide up that time?

The California State Bar is made up of three sections: essay, performance test and multiple choice or MBE. The first day starts with a three-hour block where the applicant must complete three essays to earn full credit for that section. Here, the examinee may choose to do any of the first three essays in any order, she may also commit as much time as she feels necessary to complete any essay. For example, an examinee may start the exam with essay number three, and only spend one half hour to complete it, leaving two and one-half hours for questions one and two. For the essay section, an equal distribution of time is one hour per essay.

After the first three hours are completed the examinee is given a one-hour break. The examinee then returns to the testing site where she is given an additional three and a half hours to complete two additional essays and a performance test. When I took the California State Bar, the performance test was a written memorandum (it can be other assignments) where the examinee must follow strict instructions for drafting said document in accordance with the law provided in the "library" given to the examinee after the break. Examinees were restricted to the law provided in the library and generally should not rely on outside substantive knowledge. Here, the applicant has free will to go about organizing her outline and reviewing the library as she saw fit. She may also have chosen to spend the bulk of her time organizing and outlining or writing the actual memorandum. Generally, an equal distribution of time was one hour of reading, one hour of outlining, and one hour to write.

Undoubtedly, as a prudent test taker you must augment your practice strategy to compensate for the change in the time allotted for the performance test. This change as of July 2017, will be a trial period for the examiners. Therefore, they have altered the performance test to allow for you to draft a complete answer. Keep this in mind when studying for this portion of the exam.

Day two is the multiple-choice section or MBE. It's two hundred multiple choice questions and administered in two, three-hour blocks. The first three hours is for the first one hundred questions followed by a one-hour break and the next three hours is for the second one hundred questions. During each section, the examinee may answer the questions in any order and spend as much time as she wants on each. For the MBE, an equal distribution of time for each question works out to be 1.8 minutes per question.

For the purposes of this book I'm not going to review time management strategies for each section and question type. That task is left for your prep course. I did give equal time allocations for each section to give you a general idea of how you can divide up your time. Certainly, as you practice each section you will learn that not all questions are created equally. The key is to use your best judgment in assessing how difficult a problem is and allocate your time accordingly. Some questions will be resolved rather quickly, others may take a bit longer and others will resolve right on time. Later, I will discuss some tricks Bar examiners use to make time an even greater foe and some tips on how to recognize and circumvent those traps. But for now, let's conclude with an exercise on familiarizing yourself with your test's administrative requirements/restrictions and macro format.

## EXERCISE FIVE
## Administrative and Format
## Critique

Now that you have seen the breakdown for the California State Bar do the same for your test. Before you take your test again you should be able to answer these questions from memory.

1. What must you bring to your exam before you can sit?
2. What items are prohibited at the exam testing site?
3. What is the total time allotted for your exam?
4. How is that time divided?
5. How many subjects does your exam cover?
6. How many sections does your exam have?
7. How much time can be devoted to each section?
8. How much time is suggested you spend on each question?
9. Are there substantive restrictions on any section?
10. Are you practicing according to these time restrictions?

### Test Interrogatories and Answer Choices

The first few areas of this chapter covered macro issues like statistics and the administration of your test.  Let's narrow our focus and discuss understanding your test's interrogatories and the answer choices for multiple choice sections.  Not all questions are created equally.  Part of your job is to discern which questions will require more time and attention than others.  Test creators are well versed in "hiding the ball" in so far as making questions read easier than they appear. Here are a few caveats for the essay section that can alarm you to the test maker's agenda.

### General vs. Specific Interrogatories

A common mistake for test takers on the essay portion of their exam is to give the question a cursory review. Test creators know this so they purposefully hide the important issues right in the question, counting on you to overlook them. They are directly testing if you can follow directions.  To avoid this trap, be diligent and scrutinize each question thoroughly.  First, determine if the call of the question is general or specific.  Let's look at this seemingly simple question. What are John Doe's rights? In this case, the hypothetical will have John engaged in an obvious legal subject like, criminal law.  John is battered by an unknown assailant in a dark alley and a high-speed police chase ensues.  The perpetrator is arrested and taken to jail, John is interviewed by the police and subsequently decides to seek your counsel. The violent context draws our minds to naturally think of John's right to prosecute his attacker, right? But the call demands that you discuss *all* of John's rights under any applicable theory of law, not just the theory that is obviously posed in the hypothetical (remember many facts can cross over into multiple subjects like crimes and torts).

What if the call of the question is specific? For example, what are Jane's equitable rights under contract law? Here the question limits you to Jane's rights under contract law so you will not discuss torts, crimes or violation of her constitutional rights. In this case Jane will have contracted for either a good or service that she must have and can only be done by one person. For example, Jane may want a wedding dress for her one and only "special" day. The test creators are purposefully making it obvious that Jane's priority it to have this specific custom dress that only one designer can make. However, do not be misguided, by hypothetical fact patterns that intentionally highlight one equitable remedy like specific performance. Although specific performance is one option do not fail to discuss other possible equitable remedies like restitution or an injunction if there are facts there to support them. Picking up these hidden points is a matter of developing a check list mentality where you spot issues based on a complete mental flow-chart of substantive law relevant to the call of the question.  Simply put, you check to determine if the issue can be discussed based on its flow chart not by what is apparent on the face of the hypothetical.

For both general and specific question types the test makers have a back-up plan just in case you have been diligent.  They know that in the grips of answering a question you can become overwhelmed with emotion or let your arrogance guide your decision making.  Also, time pressure can play a pivotal role in allowing the call of the question to be lost in your overall analysis. For these reasons, the hypotheticals associated with the call of the question may be emotionally charged, deceptively short or tediously long.

### Emotionally charged hypotheticals

Topics such as race, rape, child molestation, gun rights, free speech and religion, stir our emotions in some way.  It may be because we identify with a group or the allegations are graphic and violent.  It could be that the correct legal analysis reaches a conclusion that conflicts with your sense of right and wrong. That may very well be, but your goal is to conduct an objective analysis and discuss all relevant issues then conclude based on the facts as applied to the substantive law.

Emotionally charged facts, tempt you to conduct your analysis and base your conclusions according to your feelings about a set of circumstances and not on your substantive knowledge. For example, John Doe a former high school swimming champion sees a paralyzed woman pleading for someone to save her drowning child in a local swimming pool. John could easily jump in and save the little girl but refuses to do so because he does not want to ruin his new haircut. What is John's liability for refusing to help the child? Could you argue these facts either way? Sure. Is John liable? Maybe, depends on the law of the jurisdiction. The point is fact patterns like this aim to tug at your heart strings to cause you to feel sympathy for the girl and her mother. Your challenge is to analyze the facts based on the applicable substantive law. Quick test, was the call of the question in my hypothetical general or specific? Did you remember to ask yourself that question?

Short hypotheticals

Do not assume the answer to a question is simple just because the hypothetical has a low word count. Often the opposite is the truth. Shorter hypotheticals inherently call for more inferences, conjecture and analysis. Here, the examiners are requiring you to fill in what is missing through your ability to read between the lines. They are testing your ability to flesh out an analysis though relevant and logical inferences. Moreover, you may be required to make reasonable assumptions to conduct your analysis thoroughly. The key to knowing what assumptions are related to a context comes from practicing essays. There are common inferences and assumptions that are associated with each subject.

Also, short hypotheticals are misleading in their appearance causing one to reasonably think that there can't be much analysis required because there aren't many facts to deal with. Do not be led astray by this visual illusion. Here, your job is to give each word *greater meaning*, this allows you to pose relevant questions based on your broad definitions, and flesh out the undertones of the hypothetical. Often, there is a hidden public policy issue underlying the fact pattern. Your goal is to spot this policy issue, discuss it within the confines of the fact pattern and come to some balanced analysis all while addressing the call of the question.

## Lengthy hypotheticals

At last the time has come for the proctor to utter those adrenaline rushing words, "You may now open your test booklet and begin your exam." You rip open the tab only to see a page and a quarter of fact pattern. What's your first reaction before you read one word? SKIP IT, I'll come back to it! Well, hold on not so fast. The test creators are playing on your heightened since of anxiety. They know you are anxious about time and about the complexity of an analysis for such a lengthy fact pattern. They want you to either skip it and be forced to rush through the facts at the end of the section or to do it first and spend too much time over analyzing leaving little time for the remaining questions.

Don't be frazzled by this visual intimidation tactic. The test examiners understand how much time you have so they will never give you a question you cannot answer competently within the time constraints. Lengthy fact patterns test your ability to organize and distinguish facts. Your job is to keep track of what is happening and place each fact in the appropriate section of your analysis. You also must categorize which facts are material, meaning crucial to the resolution of your issue from facts that are peripheral. The material facts are to be discussed first and given more scrutiny while collateral facts are used to fill in gaps or emphasize an argument.

Mistakes associated with lengthy fact patterns are fact omissions, spending too much time analyzing non-essential facts and running out of time over analyzing. You can prevent these mistakes by thoroughly outlining your issues and facts before you start to write your essay. Generally, once everything is organized the analysis is much easier because you spend less time rereading the facts.

## "Give Them What They Want!"

To sum up what we have discussed in this section, first quickly identify how the test takers are trying to influence you with their formatting tricks and secondly *give them what they want.* The first part should happen quickly. Before you start to read the call of the question give the entire hypothetical and question(s) a glance then ask yourself, "what kind of problem is this format wise?" Is it long, short or medium length? Do you see a lot of exclamation points and bold words? Form a preliminary judgment about what you see. For example, you may see a quarter page length hypothetical with uppercase words and a general interrogatory at the end. You can then assume this essay may not be as simple as it looks. You may have to make assumptions and it may have facts that cross-over into multiple subjects. Next, read the call and the fact pattern and ask yourself, again, "what kind of question is this?" Is it emotionally charged? Are their multiple parties and a lot of details? You may write on your scratch paper, "Don't let emotions influence your analysis or organization." Both steps should take no more than 2 to 3 minutes depending on the length of the fact pattern.

Completing both steps is a great way to familiarize yourself with the context before you attempt to take on the question. It's the fact that you are taking a timed test whose grade will determine if you are licensed to practice is what causes the rush into answering the question. You will be far more prepared to competently answer the test's questions if you first take a little time to, "size them up." Even when we are cognizant of certain tricks the test makers will play we can still be susceptible to them if we are not consciously aware of them as we write out the answer. One way to be sure you won't become victim to their tricks is to incorporate a trick spotting mechanism into your test taking strategy.

"Give them what they want." I've heard this mantra over the years from countless colleagues and tutors. But what does it mean? Well it means something different for each test taker. Some don't put in enough study time. Others put in too much, while some have the right quantity but low quality.

Firstly, you must know the standard. This means you must know what they want before you can give it to them. Knowing what the test takers are looking for comes from, you guessed it, institutional memory. Your course tutors should know exactly the format and language the Bar graders need to see. For the Bar, no grader wants to read informal tone, slang, incorrect spelling or egregious grammatical errors. She does not want to read misplaced terms of art, unnecessary legal jargon or irrelevant verbose opinions that do not add to your analysis. If your test is graded by a person, meaning other than a multiple choice scantron, generally that person will not have much time to devote to your individual test. Therefore, it is your job to give them exactly what they are looking for to give you points, nothing less nothing more.

Here's an example. Imagine that you are Xena Z, studying to be an employment law attorney for victims of wage discrimination and unfair hiring practices. After three years of law school you are finally sitting for your Bar exam. You open your test booklet and the last question is a fact pattern about Joe Q. Public, a wealthy board member of a multi-national manufacturing corporation. Joe is being sued for laundering illegal drug funds through the corporate books as well as sexual harassment of his single mother secretary who for years he has underpaid. You are Joe's defense attorney.

Unsure what to type you freeze up and initially become unwilling to advocate for someone whom you find morally repugnant. You hastily assume that the secretary's claim against your client deserves more attention than the money laundering allegation because sexual harassment is an issue you feel strongly about and frankly more interesting. Enchanted at the opportunity to express your convictions about wage discrimination you get confused and begin to argue that the secretary's complaint for damages is justified.

After a few minutes of nail biting and toe tapping you eventually clear your head, give your best effort and finish just in the nick of time. Then suddenly, you hear the proctor say, "TIME IS UP." You immediately close your test booklet and take a breath. You think for a second how you masterfully weaved the facts and law together on the sexual harassment and wage discrimination issues. You made distinctions between common law and statutory law, you argued an exception that applied to one of the relevant rules of law, you argued fairly for both sides and came to a clear conclusion. You even found the time to add a paragraph on the effect this case would have on real world public policy. Upon your initial reflection you think, "The grader will have no choice but to give me a 75 or better!"

That was the last essay of the 1st section so it's lunch time. You go to a near-by sandwich shop and order a club sandwich, chips and water. You sit calmly and before you can take the first bite you wonder, "Did I address the money laundering question thoroughly?" Then another question pops in your mind, "I was defense counsel right?" I concluded that my client should not be liable but I spent so much time discussing public policy, was that even relevant? Will I get points for that?" You think of a few more miscues and look up to realize 45 minutes have passed since lunch began. You have eaten 1/3$^{rd}$ of your sandwich, no chips and your water is unopened. You have fifteen minutes to return to the test site and prepare for the second three-hour session. In a panic, you wrap up your lunch and speed walk to the site where you are discombobulated and somewhat ticked that you may have bombed an essay on the exact subject you are studying to practice. And then the proctor says, "You may now begin the second half of the day."

Scenarios such as this have happened to the best of us, so don't worry. And for the purposes of our hypothetical, Xena does pass the Bar. How did Xena pass in the face of her uncertainties? Xena effectively put aside her initial bias against Joe. She argued defenses for each charge and allegation. She humanized her client while attacking the complaining witness' (the secretary) credibility. Most importantly Xena showed how the plaintiff failed to prove the elements of her cause of action while proving up the elements of her client's affirmative defenses. On the contrary, Xena did not receive any extra points for her public policy rant because it was not relevant to the call of the question. It did however add to her anxiety and cut into her time for a post analysis review and spell check.

The point of our exercise in imagination is to remember that your goal is to give the test graders what they want. We do this by sizing up the question first. Ask questions like, what issue does this fact support? Is this question emotionally charged? Does my outline present an application of fact to law or is it just my organized opinion on an issue I have strong feelings about? Before you begin to write out your answer make sure your outline contains analyses that are eligible for points. Fortunately, Xena, notwithstanding her public policy tangent, gave the graders what they wanted. There was another issue Xena faced during her lunch break which we will discuss in a later chapter. Can you think of what I'm referring to?

## Multi-state Bar Exam (MBE)

There is a myriad of test strategies for solving multiple choice questions, but I'll leave that for your prep course. Here, I'm going to discuss some general rules of thumb that can apply to any multiple-choice examination.

While the key to the essay portion is to give them what they want, for multiple- choice exams selecting the "best" answer is your goal. What does this mean? It means that there can be more than one right answer, however, of the two, maybe three right answers only one is the best. I can tell you from my experience improving my MBE score with each consecutive exam that you learn which answer is the best through practice. Reviewing the answer choices in the back of the book will give you the reasoning behind why the examiners have determined why choice A is better than choice B or C. Usually, the best answer is the choice that resolves the issue considering the context described in the fact pattern.

The committee that creates the multiple-choice section for your exam uses similar slights of hand like in the essays to intimidate and confuse you or influence your analysis and ultimate answer choice. Here are some common multiple-choice tricks.

### Context specific answers

No matter how much analyzing you do the only way to be sure you have the correct answer is familiarity with contexts. To become familiar with hundreds of contexts you must practice and review literally *thousands* of questions.

## Not all questions are created equally

Some questions will be dispensed with quickly, others may take a bit longer, some will resolve right on time (heard this before?). Here, the examiners are banking on your neurotic compulsion to try and get every question correct at all costs. If you adopt this attitude then they have won and you will likely do poorly on this section of the exam. Usually all multiple questions are given equal weight point wise (check your specific exam) therefore, just because you spend 5 extra minutes on an especially difficult question and get it correct does not mean you will be awarded extra points. Examinees who do this tend to run out of time and then must speed through the end of the exam or guess the last set of questions to avoid leaving them blank.

If you run into a question that appears particularly easy and you are confident in your analysis and answer, believe you have selected the correct answer and move on. Conversely, if you come across a difficult question do your best within your time restraints, pick the answer you think is best and move on. Even if you misdiagnose a few questions as either too simple or too hard in the end it all tends to balance out. Your focus on the multiple-choice section is to ensure that you give each question its due time and consideration.

## Putting the best answer choice last

If the multiple-choice portion of your exam is split into two parts you may feel like one half was more difficult than the other. For my final round at the Bar I finished the first hour of the MBE well within time. I felt sure I'd done a good job due to my pace and overall feeling. But the second half for whatever reason seemed a bit more difficult. I didn't finish quite as fast as the first half and the questions just seemed harder in general. I know fatigue certainly played a part in the increased difficulty, but there was certainly a noticeable discrepancy in complexity between the questions in the two sections.

You may notice toward the end of the MBE that the subject matter gets more difficult. For example, the first 100 questions may end with short to midsize torts and criminal law questions, whereas, the second half ends with lengthy contracts and evidence questions. Toward the end of the test the examiners know you are tired. They may place longer more difficult questions at the back end to test your endurance and concentration. Moreover, the earlier answer choices like A and B, are drafted to be attractive and appeal to your general sense of right and wrong. The order of the answer choices is designed this way to exploit your fatigue. At this vulnerable moment, the examiners place the best answer second to last or last. This technique tests your patience and tempts you to choose one of the first two choices.

## More Multiple-Choice Advice

Undoubtedly, examiners use subject specific nuances and tricks specific to your exam to keep you off balance, but the key to any multiple-choice exam is timing. Proper timing is achieved with confident analysis, picking the best answer and moving on. Timing's worst enemy is second guessing. Do not second guess yourself.

Understand that you must practice an inordinate amount of questions to familiarize with the multitude of contexts you will encounter. Don't be intimidated by the quantity, just focus on *effort*. Make a point to practice questions from a variety of sources. You may hear company A has the best practice questions or company X's questions are too easy. Do not let such conjecture misguide you. Each source's set of questions has its own unique value and will aid in your preparation. In short, they all complement each other so practice as many different question types from as many different sources as you can.

Review all the questions you have practiced, including the questions you get correct. Why? Practicing the questions you get correct allows you to see when your analysis and the examiners' are along the same lines. This bolsters your confidence and helps sustain your motivation. It ensures that you are using the same analysis and reasoning that the examiners use to come to their conclusions. Also, it is a great way reinforce your substantive knowledge and highlights your strong areas.

Obviously, you must also correct questions you get incorrect. During this practice stage you learn the most. Correcting incorrect answers points out your weak areas which allows you to tailor your substantive review accordingly. Here, you can see the flaws in your reasoning, analysis and substantive knowledge. Also, take notes of your common mistakes and patterns of illogical reasoning. Certainly, it will be very frustrating correcting wrong answers, but the quick remedy for this feeling is to realize that it's supposed to be difficult. The prep MBE books would not be doing their job if during your preparation you got every question correct. It is perfectly acceptable, even expected, for you to initially get 30 to 40 percent of multiple-choice questions incorrect. Therefore, after a particularly difficult practice session take your frustration and focus it on your review so that you do not repeat the mistakes you have identified and worked to correct.

## Performance Test

Understanding the performance test requires competency in 2 key areas: following directions/finding the Rosetta stone and organization/outlining.

One common tactic examiners use to confuse test takers on the performance test is to hide the ball. The examiners usually inform the applicant how the assignment will be graded according to percentages. For example, the argument section of the memo may count for 70 percent while the accompanying statement of facts may count for the remaining 30 percent. This information is sometimes given at the very beginning of the file on the first few pages buried among the boilerplate instructions. This rouse fools those examinees who are anxiously waiting to get to the meat of the file and consequently skip or give the initial directions a cursory review.

Read the first pages thoroughly while scanning for information on grading procedures, limitations on applicable law and the like. Take note of what you spot and incorporate that information into your overall strategy/outline. Referencing our example above, if you notice that 70 percent of the points make up the argument section of your memo the outline should reflect a greater allocation of time and analytical detail to that section. The subsequent statement of facts worth the remaining 30 percent should not be given as much time and detail as the argument section.

You may even consider drafting the argument section first even though traditional writing methods call for the statement of facts to be written first. There are applicants who skip or glance over the boilerplate instructions and do not outline their analysis correctly or properly allocate their time. This behavior results in valuable points being lost on the performance exam.

The directions for the assignment are outlined in the memo. Usually it's a letter from a senior attorney advising her associate on what type of document must be drafted. The directions must be read very carefully. The key is to draft only what is assigned, nothing less and nothing more. For example, a memorandum of points and authorities generally includes a statement of facts. Many law students know this so when they read that the assignment is to draft a memo they assume it includes a statements-of-facts. For the purposes of the Bar exam this is not the case.

Do not assume anything belongs in a performance test memo just because it is traditionally included. Oftentimes, the senior attorney will, in passing, mention that certain parts of the memo have already been drafted or are being left for another attorney to complete. It is your job to scrutinize the directions strictly so that you do not overlook these limitations. Applicants who misunderstand the directions in this way tend to run out of time. So, avoid drafting unnecessary parts of the document. Their analysis in key areas often suffer due to the stress caused by time pressure. Also, the applicant may lose credibility and ultimately points for being unable to follow or understand directions clearly.

A quick story. During college, I worked as an administrative assistant and legal courier for a prominent civil law firm. I had the opportunity to speak with the partners on occasion. I can recall a conversation with a senior partner who explained to me the probationary period many new associates must endure before they are assured job security. He told me, "Curtis, we hired a young man a few years ago who was highly intelligent. He graduated top of his class and was very ambitious. His first assignment was to draft a small portion of a motion we needed to file. And instead of doing what we told him, he went out and did extra research and turned in a fully drafted motion. So, we had to let him go." I looked into the senior partner's eyes after he told me the story, I could sense that he thought highly of the young associate and regretted having to fire him. But this is the nature of the business and the same principle applies to the Bar. The lesson here is, you must do what you are told, no more no less.

Now that you understand how crucial following the directions can be to your time management and the impression you make on the grader, you must turn your attention to using the correct legal analysis. When resolving any legal issue, the analysis must proceed according to the proper framework. Elements must be addressed and questions answers in a logical order before one can come to a well-reasoned conclusion. Often the key will be hidden in the library among the statutes and case law. This is the proverbial Rosetta stone that is the key to your legal analysis.

One trick the examiners use is to present you with a partial framework at the very beginning of the library. Here, the applicant reads through the first case and realizes, "Ah ha!" I have found applicable case law and elements. The examinee begins her outline early to maximize time through multi-tasking (outlining and reading at the same time). She then reads on only to find that this case law is incomplete (partial framework). Now the outline that she has created must be augmented. Moreover, say an applicant finds her case law early on and creates her outline. She reads further into the library only to find out that the law has been overturned. Now that outline must be totally scrapped because it can no longer be used to support any arguments. The best way to overcome this pitfall is to simply take note of the locations of all potential rules of law. Be patient and read the entire file before you begin to outline. Once you have noted all your applicable rules of law, go back and sift through them. Scrap those that are incomplete or inapplicable and incorporate the proper rules into your outline.

While searching for the key to your issue don't be fooled by the source that provides the key. Law students are expected to know the hierarchy of precedent, meaning you must know which law is given more consideration over another. Here, the examiners may place a comprehensive framework under the heading Restatement of XYZ law while there is a cursory legal analysis of the same issue outlined in a case (case law). Do not be fooled into writing yourself out of the question by using the cursory analytical framework of the case law and dismissing the Restatement analysis just because Restatements are not binding. You job here is to analyze both. Give attention to the case law analysis first while offering the Restatement as a secondary advisory authority.

Failure to take note of the court's jurisdiction also causes confusion. Again, we are referring to precedent hierarchy. Law students must know that U.S Supreme Court holdings supersede all other law, next are Federal Circuit Courts, State Supreme Courts and finally the State Courts of Appeal. When analyzing any given issue addressed by two or more courts the precedent always lies with the highest court of the group. Therefore, you must take note of the court's jurisdiction and give its case law due deference.

Next, let's turn our attention to outlining and organization. A common mistake for many applicants is reading and outlining at the same time or even worse, reading, outlining and writing simultaneously to save time. The decision to either read the file first or library first depends on the test taker. Some like to read the cases first get an idea of the law then read the file to understand the facts. Others find it more comfortable to read the file first, understand the facts then read the library. It's really a matter of comfort and preference. The point is to *read through it all before you begin to outline and outline it all before you begin to write.*

A good rule of thumb is to section off your tasks into compartments and work within the confines of that task until complete. Here is one suggested course of action. Read the boilerplate directions first and take note of any valuable information. Then read the file first while only taking notes on the facts. Then move on to the library and read the cases and statutes. Categorize them as either supportive (positive) or in opposition (negative) to your argument. Next, outline your analysis based on your notes from all sections. Finally write your memo from your outline. Like with all strategies you may be conscious of what to do, but you must practice it repeatedly to ensure that you execute properly under time pressure.

The performance test is not always a memo of points and authorities sometimes you will be asked to draft an opening or closing statement. The examiners know that as a law student you have very little to no trial experience. However, you are expected to know the fundamentals of trial preparation including drafting opening and closing statements.

This task involves basic legal skills like applying facts to law, asserting affirmative defenses, citing presumptions and burdens of proof, story-telling and ultimately being persuasive while advocating in your client's best interests. Usually, drafting an opening statement will be part of a larger assignment and worth only a fraction of the available points.

To keep you on your toes the examiners may make the opening and closing worth exactly half or close to half of all total points, putting you in a bind over which section to give priority to. Do not panic if this situation occurs. Simply realize that your outline must reflect a balanced approach considering time and analysis for each section. Here is a list of elements that most openings and closings should address.

- Properly address jury.
- Present a compelling theory of the case in a light favorable to your client.
- Establish the theme of the case.
- Address the elements of law and how you as prosecutor has met each element required for a conviction or as defense counsel proved your affirmative defense.
- How the prosecution has failed to meet its burden.
- Preempt the opposing side's arguments.
- A clear conclusion stating why the defendant is guilty or not guilty/ why plaintiff should be awarded claim.
- State the opposition's burden of proof.
- Call into question the credibility of opposing counsel's evidence and witnesses.

By no means is this an exhaustive list but it's a start. Can you think of other factors that a good opening and closing should address? Now that we have a better understanding of how the examiners try and trip us up with slights of hand. Let's delve deeper into other psychological challenges that you must overcome when preparing for an entrance and/or exit exam.

### The Hidden Psychological Exam

I can safely say that if you have made it to this point, (being a Bar applicant) you can consider yourself smart. And the Bar examiners know this. Therefore, to create a competitive exam, the committee must give you a gambit of trials that test beyond substantive knowledge and legal analysis. Some non-obvious obstacles are the psychological challenges you must face before and during your preparation and exam.

Consider the California State Bar's reputation as one of the most difficult Bars in the country. How does this make you feel as an applicant? Does it intimidate you? Does it make you feel like it's unfair that other states have, "easier" Bars? What about the other side? Do you get a sense of pride in taking the one of the hardest attorney admittance exam in the country? Undoubtedly, the California Bar is difficult. It's two full days and tests federal law and state law distinctions in some subjects. And other state Bars also have their own unique hurdles. However, it's obvious that even before you begin to take the test, the Bar's reputation has some effect on you and how you choose to prepare.

Let's consider its name, "The Bar". When you think of a Bar you may imagine a line you must get over. You may see it as something you must reach. Others may consider it a prohibition or something that keeps people out. No matter how you interpret the moniker, "Bar exam", its name will have some effect on you and how you choose to prepare for it. Again, even before taking the test, you are subtlety being influenced to perceive the exam as difficult. Couldn't they have just named it the attorney's licensing exam? No. It's called, "The Bar." Oh, scary, right?

Let's review the pass/fail statistics for the California Bar. On average around 50% pass in July and 40% pass in February. Do these numbers bring your confidence down? For July is the glass half full or half empty? What about February? Will you avoid taking the exam in February on the sole fact that fewer than half of examinees pass every year? Do you spend time trying to figure out why so few examinees pass, or why more pass in July than in February? Have you spent time analyzing the variations in pass/fail percentages for each administration? If you answered yes to ANY of these questions, then you do not have the proper mindset for properly preparing to pass the Bar. You are falling prey to the hidden psychological challenge inherent in this exam. In short, DO NOT

CONCERN YOURSELF WITH THESE ISSUES.

Let's move on to the applicant pool. Population wise, hundreds of people take the Bar each year and many of them are from top tier law schools. They graduated summa cum laude, were editors of their school's Bar review and graduated in their classes' top tenth percentile. Very intimidating, right?

And finally, the day of the exam you bear witness to the hundreds of students funneling into a convention center or fancy hotel. They all have expensive laptops and designer eyewear looking as if they have already litigated a trial to jury verdict. Some of these applicants are wearing their Stanford, Harvard, Yale or NYU School of Law hoodie. They must know everything, right? Absolutely not!

Those applicants must face the same academic, psychological and physical challenges as everyone else. The laptop, sweater and glasses do nothing to aid them in passing the exam. I'm sure you understand the point I'm making but somehow the atmosphere that surrounds the Bar on exam day is its own psychological challenge. Do not allow the volume of applicants, their appearance or the competitive nature of the exam psych you out in any way.

## Burnout and Frustration

The next sections are related to a two-headed beast I like to call, "burnout and frustration." These events are not mutually exclusive meaning they can happen simultaneously, therefore, you want to avoid them both at all costs. The basic formula? Frustration leads to rash acts and those rash acts produce burnout, once you burnout your production drops and may lead to outright giving up.

Frustration is at the core of our dilemma; it's where it all starts. Many things in our lives cause frustration but we must distinguish that which is caused by everyday life and that which is caused by the psychological roller coaster that is exam preparation. First, do not allow the drama in your life to frustrate your practice or substantive review. For example, your roommate is particularly annoying, car breaking down, bills to pay, parents on your back, work environment unsatisfying, family life somewhat dysfunctional, etc. These are all legitimate reasons for general frustration, however, they will always exist, so do not let them interfere with your schedule. There will never be a perfect time to study for the Bar. Never postpone preparing for a test just because you are experiencing some trivial inconvenience. Use your best judgment to determine if what is going on in your life is so traumatic that you can justifiably put off seriously preparing to pass your exam.

The best approach is to realize that you must learn to shut these general nuisances off during your study hours then return to resolving them after you are done for the day. If you cannot seem to shake off the frustrations of your daily life before you begin to study for the day, then TAKE SOME TIME OFF! Generally, two or three hours just resting or doing nothing will suffice. I'm not suggesting you take a week or two off.

For example, it's early November and Sam is just starting his preparation for the February Bar. It's football season and Sam is upset because his favorite team isn't doing so well in the standings. His mother is planning a big Thanksgiving dinner this year and expects Sam to bring his girlfriend to meet her and his father for the first time. After working a long Monday shift as an insurance sales-man, Sam gets a call from his girlfriend. She says that things just aren't working out. Sam is taking too long to pass the Bar and become a lawyer and she is tired of coming in second to his ultimate career goal. It's now 9:00pm and Sam has a 2-hour block dedicated to completing his torts flow chart. Sam really wants to study because he is determined to get off to a good start this time around. Tired from work, anxious about Thanksgiving and frustrated with his relationship,

Sam puts his head in his hands and doesn't know what to do.

Should Sam:
(A)    Put it all behind him and study.
(B)    Call his girlfriend back and try to work it out.
(C)    Go to bed for the night.
(D)    All the above.

Which did you choose? To answer this question, we must remember some of the tips we discussed earlier, we should consider the best answer and not make any assumptions. Let's review. Choice (A) is good but due to the circumstances it may be impossible for Sam to do. He may be able to temporarily put it behind him for the night but these same issues will still be around when it's time for Sam to study again. Moreover, Sam's study time will likely be less productive because he has other things on his mind.

Choice (B) is also reasonable. If Sam can work it out with this girlfriend he can presumably get her to come to the Thanksgiving dinner at his parent's home, thus, resolving two issues. However, the context in the hypothetical suggests that Sam and his girlfriend have just talked and could not come to a resolution. And Sam is still frustrated, so calling back will likely lead to another argument not a compromise or solution. (B) is not the best choice. Answer (C) is enticing because Sam does need to calm down and get a good night's sleep. But choice (C) alone fails to address the issues causing Sam's frustration. Through the process of elimination, we are left with answer choice (D) All the above. Wouldn't it be best for Sam to take a course of action containing all 3 choices?

Let's imagine Sam hanging up with his girlfriend and putting his head in his hands. He then decides to call it a day and gets a good night's rest. Because he went to bed early he wakes up early refreshed and decides to outline his torts flowchart that morning and makes sure to send his girlfriend a gift. Later that week he calls his girlfriend back and they reconcile agreeing to give it a fresh start at his family's Thanksgiving dinner. Whew! This is a simplified but useful example, note how you can avoid frustration with a balanced approached to scheduling your life and prep time. Why did Sam need to take such a course of action? Well you need tools to help overcome life's frustrations so that you do not do anything rash leading to burnout. The number one cause of poor preparation for exams like the Bar is burnout and frustration. You want to avoid them like the plague. Had Sam let his frustration get the best of him he may have made a rash decision and put himself on a path to burnout.

Frustration comes in many forms when preparing for a high-pressure exam. Consider the anxiety associated with concentrating too much on the quantity of subject matter, the technical practice required for competence, the overall time commitment and the inability to manage emotional highs and lows when performance fluctuations occur. Be sure you are prepared to accept those challenges and put in the work to overcome them.

# Accepting the Challenge

The California State Bar is undoubtedly one of the most difficult licensing exams of any profession. Not just for the variety and depth of black letter law you must memorize but also the test's format requires an applicant to be practiced at applying the law to multiple legal issues under time pressure. Many repeat takers underestimate either one or both prerequisites. Why? Because frankly, it's intimidating. Just imagine having to recall three years worth of information at the drop of a dime, for some it's just easier to ignore. But, let me reassure you that you are not required to memorize everything you learned in law school to pass the Bar. You must memorize enough substantive material to exhibit competence, not perfection and you must be diligent in accepting that fact. For others reading this book who are not taking a Bar exam, your test likely has similar memorization and analytical requirements, therefore, the advice given here applies to you also.

Considering the approximately fourteen subjects the Bar may test on, the amount of pure information you must have memorized is substantial. During your Bar preparation you may find yourself outlining black letter law or researching an issue in a hornbook or treatise and think to yourself "does the Bar really expect me to know every issue in this much detail?" And the answer is No! This does not suggest that you can pass with just memorizing the bare minimum. You must have a firm grip on the flow of all subjects and the fundamental rules of law required for resolving any given hypothetical fact pattern. However, do not concern yourself with the volume of information. Just thinking about attempting to memorize every legal precedent gives me severe anxiety.

Instead, here and now *consciously accept the fact that you must commit to a sustained effort to memorize as much as you can until your final day of preparation.* Your goal is to shift your focus from the amount of information you must memorize to the quality of the effort you put forth in memorizing as much of the information as you possibly can up until your final day of preparation.

When I first took the Bar, I'd decided to self-study. Since I did not have access to the institutional wisdom of a prep course I didn't have a good sense of how much black letter law I needed to memorize. Like some first timers I underestimated how much I needed to know and did not commit to pushing myself to memorize as much information as I was capable of. As a result, during my first round at the Bar there were several issues whose analysis required rules of law I could not recall. To make matters worse, one essay called for an exception that I was just simply unaware of. My deficiency in black letter law reared its ugly head during the multiple-choice section as well. Take heed that lack of substantive knowledge will have a detrimental effect on every section of your exam in one way or another. Why? Because your substantive knowledge supplies the rules of law that connect to relevant facts to create a competent analysis. And undoubtedly each section of your exam will call for you to make some sort of judgment based on the rules associated with practicing your profession.

I'm sure that some of you have heard that Bar graders don't care about reciting exact rules or that it is perfectly acceptable to "make up" a rule if you don't know it. Well, that myth may hold true for some graders, while other graders may not appreciate fabricated elements, especially for fundamental issues they feel all law students should know. For example, the elements of negligence in torts or formation in contracts are taught during the first year and by the time a law student takes the Bar, employers, clients and Bar graders will expect students to have the elements to these issues memorized. The point is that the "make up" a rule method should be reserved as a last resort.

Along with the under-estimators are the over-estimators who needlessly clamor over every rule, exception and legal nuisance. Overestimating causes an applicant to spend too much time reviewing outlines to memorize every single little detail. Common sense suggests that it is impossible for the human brain to have every testable legal precedent memorized such that one can access any given rule at random during a timed examination. However, many of us try to do so and our neurotic behavior earns us days or even weeks of wasted time trying to "memorize it all."

I can recall one of my Bar prep classmates laboring over the various types of criminal conspiracies that could be tested on the Bar. I'd like you to imagine her standing next to you and literally panicking over whether a criminal conspiracy requires an, "overt act or a substantial step" in the furtherance of the target offense. And I was certainly not immune to her panic. It quickly spread and like a virus and infected me. I can remember thinking, "Well those elements are very similar. Will the grader think less of my essay for citing an element inaccurately? What if that distinction is tested on the multiple-choice section? Hmmm, I'd better review my outline again to make sure."

I look back at my old thought process and see that I was caught in the grip of overzealousness.

Not to suggest that a quick review of an element or buzz word/phrase isn't appropriate occasionally, but, failing to use exact language when describing an element will not make or break you. What will break you is wasting time repeatedly reviewing legal minutia every time you can't recite a buzz word or phrase verbatim.

Both the under and over estimation of how much black letter law needs to be memorized are mistakes that can prevent you from using your time more efficiently. Where does the median value of substantive knowledge lie? That minimum black letter competence can be achieved through (1) an initial comprehensive substantive review (generally by completing a thorough flow chart for each subject). And, (2) the completion of a practice regime containing all phases (MBE, Essay, Performance Test) designed to cover your exam's highly tested issues. Once you have completed the proper practice schedule you will have memorized enough information necessary to answer enough questions to exhibit competency. *In sum, focus on sustaining your maximum effort through the end of your preparation. Do not worry yourself with trying to memorize every nuance.*

Your exam is designed to test several fine line details. You cannot expect to ignore wholesale the small distinctions that your exam will test. Rely on the institutional memory of a professional course to expose you to the details that are commonly tested. Do not spend your time reviewing past exams attempting to catalogue which details are commonly tested. That strategy is a waste of your most valuable resource, time. Remember you have a limited amount of time to review your substantive material once. Complete a full substantive review once so that you can allot the bulk of your time to what really prepares you to pass your exam, that being practicing your technique.

### Accepting the Amount of Technical Practice Required

In our world technique is defined as how one chooses to approach an exam on the macro level and how one choses to go about analyzing and solving each question type on a micro level. Ultimate success requires practicing technique on both a macro and micro level. Therefore, it is necessary for you to track the statistical data produced from your practice exams and monitor your effort to determine where your technique needs work.

To properly prepare for the California State Bar you must practice a minimum number of MBEs, essays and performance tests and frankly it's *a lot*. Doing so many practice questions has a two-fold benefit. First, it familiarizes you with the hundreds of contexts you will encounter on your exam and second it repeatedly puts your technique to the test. This slowly sharpens your skills so you can perform under time pressure. Therefore, no matter how you divide it up you're going to have to do more practice questions than you are comfortable with.

There is no magic number, say for example doing 3000 MBEs that will guarantee a passing score. However, somewhere along the way you will hit a tipping point or peak performance, and this is the number that you are striving for. Since everyone has varying levels of academic acumen there is no way for me to quantify your exact number. In short, do not worry about if you have done enough practice questions to pass. The key is to do so many that you reach your peak. So how do you know when you have reached your personal peak?

Make sure you complete *all* the assignments given to you during your prep class. If you are self -studying with a personal regimen then the number of questions you do should make you uncomfortable. You are going to have to sweat a little if you want to get in enough questions to memorize the requisite amount of substantive law and become familiar with all the testable issues and various contexts while being able to analyze them to a complete solution. Also, use your intuition based on a few weeks of practice and your overall law school experience to sense which subjects, issues or sub-issues you have trouble analyzing or are unfamiliar with. Once you can consistently analyze and solve problems in a methodical and almost mechanical fashion then you know that you are nearing your peak.

Make it a point to do an honest self-assessment. Do not fall into the trap of thinking you can remember enough when the time comes so you don't need to study subject X. Or you may be thinking the opposite, that you don't know anything at all, so you have to do an absurd amount of substantive review and practice questions for a subject you've passed in law school. Be honest with yourself. If you don't know it review it, practice it and then move on. If your study regimen is exhaustive, you will see the same issues and context multiple times. If you are confident with a subject or issue the same process applies, review, practice and move on. Don't rely on past performance or familiarity to carry you through on your exam. Everything needs to be refreshed, even the subjects you already feel comfortable with.

As I stated earlier, during my first round at the Bar I did not do enough practice questions. The cause was not due to a lack of effort, but a refusal to come to terms with how many questions were required to achieve competency. I self -studied and figured a few hundred MBEs, some essays and a few performance tests would prepare me for the Bar. Looking back, I was clearly delusional because the MBE practice book I used contained over 1000 questions. I fooled myself into thinking that the practice books contained so many questions to appease over-achievers. In my mind, I thought there was no way I had to do all those questions just to pass a test. I spent three months reviewing only what I thought I needed to know and practicing just enough questions to give myself a false sense of security.

After not passing with my first effort, I did a lot more questions. More MBEs, more essays, more performance tests and undoubtedly, I wasted more time outlining. Yet I earned nearly the same total scaled score as I did the first time. I thought, "Oh my God. What went wrong? This cannot be!" I studied so much harder, did so many more practice questions and I earned the same score. It was after this attempt I learned that mindlessly doing hundreds of practice questions will not improve your score. Failing the first time forced me to accept the fact that I needed to do a greater quantity of practice questions. Point being, doing large amounts of practice questions will not improve your scores unless you have a proven strategy and a grader to point out your analytical mistakes so you do not repeat them.

By my fifth attempt I was not concerned with how many questions I practiced. I was, however, obsessed with the *quality* of my review. I learned that it was more productive to practice 15 multiple choice questions under time pressure with a thorough review for one hour rather than do 100 questions with no review and just an answer check for one and a half hours. Difference being a deeper understanding of 15 contexts, rules, issues and testing slights of hand over the false sense of security gained from knowing you did 100 questions.

Take a minute, think about your last preparation, could you have done more practice questions? If yes, how many more? If your quantity was sufficient, rate the quality. Were you doing tons of practice questions mindlessly or did you try to review the analytical process you used to choose your answer?

## Expect Your Performance to Fluctuate

Generally, you will take three to six months for Bar prep and along the way there will be times when you will answer most questions competently. You will find yourself scoring seventy percent and higher on your MBE practice tests and your essays and performance tests will come back from your grader with scores of seventy or better (You do have a grader, don't you?). Then, the pendulum will swiftly swing and your scores may drop back down to 60 percent or even lower. When this happens it's only natural for you to become frustrated. Here are a few tools to help avoid the frustration associated with performance fluctuations.

Number one, know that variances in performance will occur. Just accept it, know that no matter how much you study before-hand you will be unable to maintain a high average score (over 70%) throughout your preparation. Being cognizant of this fact prepares you emotionally for when the time comes. For example, a race car driver memorizes every curve and turn of a specific course before she takes to the track for a competitive race. She knows where to let off the gas, when to break and when to hit the throttle at each apex to get around the course in the fastest time. If she prepares this way then no turn is ever a surprise, sharp or otherwise.

Our situation is a bit different, but we can learn from the race car driver's mentality. You are never going to know when your practice scores will fall or rise. You may have a general sense of which subjects are more troublesome but so many factors determine why we perform well or not it's difficult to predict exactly when you will fall off or pick back up. Therefore, just know that your scores will fall and ultimately rise again. If you keep this fact in mind, when it occurs you will not be surprised. Like the prepared race car driver, you will know that this turn too shall pass.

We can learn and improve our preparation technique by practicing coping mechanisms like reminding ourselves that performance lulls are expected. We withhold discouraging remarks and refrain from chastising ourselves for past academic shortcomings. We do remind ourselves that encountering new issues, contexts, rules of law, exceptions and the like is a good thing because it means we are broadening our substantive knowledge and ultimately learning more. We hold firm to the confidence we have built up thus far and know that the lull will pass. Understanding that performance swings are expected, and recurring is a key to success.

So how do you create the right mindset to cope with a three to six-month time commitment and the bi-polar nature of licensing exam preparation? Understand that you are human, and your emotions have a great impact on your endurance. When you are doing well, what happens? You feel good, your endorphins are surging, you can't wait to practice more questions and your confidence is through the roof. In the words of Bob Hull, "that may be all to the good" but there is a dark side to this upswing. Beware, as your confidence may turn into cockiness, and your desire to practice may turn into an arrogant belief that you've mastered a subject. Trust me, no matter what your scores average out to be on a section you will never become so good that you do not need to continue practicing until the final few days before your exam.

Every year the Bar examiners update the exam with new tricks, slights of hand, uncommonly tested issues, new legal precedent and unfamiliar contexts. When things are going well, don't become complacent. Seek out practice books that are different from the ones you are currently using, this will give you a variety of contexts you need to stay challenged. As you work through each book you will find that some publisher's questions are generally more challenging for you. If this is the case, GREAT! Try and figure out why XYZ book's questions are more difficult than ABC book's questions. With this level of understanding you will be able to efficiently distinguish between "easy" questions from difficult questions on the essay and M.B.E sections of the Bar. Once you can distinguish accurately a question's difficulty you will be able to determine how much time you should devote to that question.

In closing, know that your performance will change overtime, expect ups and downs so when it happens you won't be surprised or become frustrated with your lack of consistency. And don't worry it's possible for your practice scores to go up and down all the way up until your final prep day. However, if you find yourself scoring consistently low toward the last few weeks on all subjects with no sign of improvement, there is cause for alarm and there is likely a fundamental flaw in your preparation that you must address immediately. Other than that extreme case do not be discouraged if you continue to average around 70% come test time. Remember your licensing exam expects competency not mastery!

### Rash Decisions and Burnout

Let's say for whatever reason you become extremely frustrated either with a life issue or with an issue that stems from prolonged study. In this state, you are likely to make a rash decision that can lead to burnout. To avoid this, let's review a few of these ill-conceived decisions so that we can be aware of what to NEVER do when we become frustrated.

The most drastic decision you can make when becoming frustrated is losing faith in your schedule, scrapping it wholesale and attempting to rev up your studying to a frantic pace. This comes up when our practice scores begin to lull and we begin to feel that our current study schedule isn't producing the results we desire. It is natural to experience the urge to abandon your schedule, when you aren't getting the scores you want, you must hold firm and be confident that the itinerary either you or your course created is sufficient (I highly recommend that you use the study schedule from a professional Bar course or tutor.)

My advice does not suggest that you cannot supplement, alter or modify your current schedule to accommodate for unforeseeable events. We all have things that pop up and demand our immediate attention. And when we become frustrated it's perfectly acceptable to take a break for a few hours or even call it day and return to our schedules refreshed. It's those of us who become infuriated and lose confidence in our course of study who are in danger of burn-out.

As you may have figured out, over studying causes academic fatigue. It may take a day or two maybe even up to a week for you to wear down. But, eventually you will be unable to sustain your frantic pace. Beware of the consequences of deciding to over study. While your scores may improve in the short term, your ability to heighten your focus as your test approaches will weaken.

Let's explore the concept of burnout. Burnout is a state of emotional, mental, and physical exhaustion caused by excessive and prolonged stress. It occurs when you feel overwhelmed and unable to meet constant demands. As the stress continues, you begin to lose interest and the motivation that led you to take on the Bar in the first place.  Burnout reduces your productivity and saps your energy, leaving you feeling increasingly helpless, hopeless, cynical, and resentful.  Other side-effects include apathy toward or an overall disinterest in substantive material, a strong desire to quit, lack of focus, poor memory and reduced mental acuity. Eventually, you may feel like you have nothing more to give.

After you've burned out some may still be able to pick up study materials, read through them, do some practice questions and review answers.  And that's fine but how much of the information are you retaining while in this fatigued state?  It's a better use of time to take a break and return refreshed.  Let's do a cursory review of what goes on physiologically in the brain when we "burnout" from prolonged mental exercise and the stress it causes.

Our nerve cells make connections with one another in tiny circuits called neural pathways. Through these pathways our body sends chemical messages using neurotransmitters.  The amino acids in our bodies create various neurotransmitters like: serotonin, acetylcholine, norepinephrine, dopamine and gamma-amino butyric acid.  Deficiencies in these neurotransmitters may cause symptoms commonly known as: depression, brain fog, low

IQ, anxiety, panic attacks, insomnia and migraines.

Biologically, neurotransmitters occur naturally in the body when we live healthy lives. It's when we add undue stress from our lifestyle or eat unhealthy foods do we develop neurotransmitter deficiencies. For example, here are some lifestyle choices and personality traits that must be avoided to prevent burnout.

## Lifestyle

- Working too much.
- Avoiding relaxation and socializing.
- Taking on too many roles.
- Failing to delegate responsibilities.
- Not getting enough sleep.
- Few supportive relationships.

## Personality

- Perfectionistic tendencies; nothing is ever good enough.
- Pessimistic view of yourself and/or the world.
- Control freak.
- Extreme type A personality.

# Setting the Mind

Before you can begin to practice the tasks outlined in your schedule you must first have the proper mindset to learn new things. Let's start with the concept of humility. Webster's Collegiate Dictionary 11th edition defines humility as: the quality or state of being humble. Ah, I see, well that gets us nowhere let's look up the root word, humble. Humble means 1: not proud or haughty: not arrogant or assertive. 2: reflecting, expressing, or offered in a spirit of deference or submission.

This is a great start for how you want to approach practicing for a licensing exam like the California State Bar. Although you have spent thousands of dollars and hundreds of hours studying for three years in law school you must realize that you know very little about taking and passing the Bar. This does not suggest that you don't have a firm grip on substantive law, issue spotting, IRAC and other legal analytical skills, it does mean that you may still need to learn how to reinforce constructive criticism, convert negative criticism into positive encouragement and be genuinely enthusiastic when you learn something new. The key is to use your repeat taker status as a spring board toward humble preparation.

Undoubtedly, the California State Bar is designed for the humble applicant to pass. One who understands that the Bar does not expect you to know every rule of law and legal nuance is poised to prepare to the best of her ability. Your goal is not to know everything, but to exhibit competence consistently. The array of testable substantive knowledge is daunting; however, the humbled applicant understands that she is not required to have memorized it all.

For example, I took a course called California Bar Tutorial with lecturer Paul Pfau. Paul would regularly assign hypothetical fact patterns to read along with interrogatories to answer. There was one moment that sticks with me. Paul assigned a torts hypothetical based on the intentional torts of assault and battery. After reading the hypothetical and answering the questions I turned in my essay. When I got my essay back I was a disappointed in the score I'd earned. I got a 65. I went about meticulously reviewing the grader's corrections and thought to myself, "These errors aren't that bad, why is the grader picking on me?" I was very upset at the time and felt like there was really no way I hadn't earned at least a 70. Some of my errors included: insufficient factual development, formatting, and tone. I could admit those mistakes, but it's not as if I'd missed an issue or forgot a rule of law. I can remember lamenting, "What does this class, want from me?" Looking back, I realize now that Paul and the Bar standard were humbling me. But what does that mean for you in this context?

It means you must offer your work product in a spirit of deference or submission as humility's formal definition suggests. To practice humility means to not only accept criticism, but to welcome it. And when the criticism concerns the fine line skills associated with proper legal analysis you must put your pride aside and understand that the errors you may perceive as insignificant often create the margin that separates those who pass from those who do not.

In hind-sight, I should have taken that essay as a lesson. Lesson being although you may feel like you have done a great job you are truly not able to judge the quality of your own work objectively. Personal bias and not knowing the grading standards are common causes of inaccurate self-assessments.

A proper mind set accepts the fact that we may need to improve in certain areas (no matter how insignificantly perceived). Let's dissect an example featuring our old friends correct spelling and proper grammar. During my first attempts at the Bar I hadn't fully developed my timing for the essays. My practice was to outline a little in the beginning, dive into the fact pattern, fill in the outline as I read then make a mad dash to complete the essay before my time was up. I give myself some credit for at least having a strategy, albeit not a very effective one.

One side effect from writing essays this way was not having much time to review my writing after it was done to spell check for spelling and grammatical errors. I can recall a few times where I'd try to spell check all three essays at the very end of the first half of the day. The result? Right in the mist of frantically clicking change or ignore for various spelling errors I'd hear the words, "TIME! Take your hands off the keyboards and turn over your booklets." I had no choice but to stop editing yet knowing that there were still spelling errors left on one or even two essays. AHHHRRGG!!! That does not make for a comfortable and confident transition into lunch time.

After being humbled I learned that having proper grammar and correct spelling throughout the exam is significant. Those two components have a great impact on the grader. Look at it this way. Imagine that you are a Bar grader and after a long day at work you decide to grade a stack of essays. You begin to read the first page and the heading states, "Forth Amendment Violation." Not bothered yet? Let's keep reading. You notice that the examinee understands the fundamentals of search and seizure analysis but the essay has an annoying recurring typo, "probably cause" instead of probable cause. You continue to read and follow the grading standard for mishaps like this. You also notice that the examinee has failed to spot a key exception to the warrant requirement, let's say its good faith reliance on the law.  Sadly, this missing this issue prevents them from earning enough points for a passing score.

If the grading standard allots points for style, writing in a lawyer-like fashion or overall impression, how do you think this grader will react?  Certainly, they would consider that the examinee is working under extreme time pressure.  However, it would be perfectly acceptable for the grader to infer that this person lacks time management skills or has failed to review her work product.  Now you have put the grader in a bind.  Analytically the grader cannot give you points if you did not spot an issue. However, always use your best efforts to earn points for style.  And sometimes those few points here and there make the difference between passing and failing.  So, what's the point?  As you begin to study, take even the smallest details seriously.  You are literally trying to prove to another professional that you are competent. In doing so you must show them that you can effectively manage time.  A telltale sign of efficient time management is the opportunity to review your work product after it's complete.

Is humility a sign of weakness? Do you feel that to convey confidence in your writing you must approach preparation like a know it all? Although confidence plays a critical role in the overall tone of your analysis, there is a psychological tight rope you must walk between confidence and arrogance. So, approach your preparation with humility.

Arrogance often comes from underestimating your opponent. You underestimate your opponent because you have failed to thoroughly assess her strengths and weaknesses. I should know. I studied for the Bar the first time with the attitude of, "all I've got to do." Translation, I was so arrogant I thought that all I needed was to brush up on a few issues because I'd passed my law school exams. I knew superficially what taking the Bar would entail but my pride and suppressed fear prevented me from looking my opponent square in the eye.

Even after not passing the first time I still didn't realize the role arrogance played in my inability to properly prepare. Why? Because I'd come so close to passing the first time. I had yet to figure out that passing the Bar is less about knowing the law generally and more about showing the grader that you understand the fine line details that separate those who barely miss the mark from those who are deemed fit to practice law.

Confidence grows from humility. The humble student understands that although she may have many skills, there is still room for improvement. Confident examinees practice at a rate where eventually they know what they can and cannot do. Thus, when the time comes they can adjust accordingly when presented with a particularly difficult task. For example, my last and final attempt at the Bar consisted of a civil procedure question regarding personal jurisdiction. I'd thoroughly studied this issue during my prep course and memorized the analytical flowchart associated with this issue.

When I read the question and interrogatory I was somewhat puzzled. The question seemed too easy, there were really no minimum contacts to argue for or against. But therein lies the test. Here, the test creators were testing my ability to answer what was in front of me and not to over answer the question. This line of thinking goes back to what Bob Johnson explained to me. You must do as you are instructed, nothing less and nothing more. This type of exam question is difficult for arrogant examinees who cannot help but to force feed more analysis into an issue than what is called for. With this question, many examinees were baited into wasting -TIME! Even if the extra analysis those over-zealous examinees wrote into the essay was marginally relevant, it will not count for many points, if any in the end. More importantly, that person has lost what they can never get back, TIME! (I cannot stress enough how important time management is for the Bar.)

In your practice have you discovered that you consistently can't do something? For example, keeping your opinion out of your analysis? The key is to learn what you can and cannot do through trial and error in practice. This will give you the confidence you need to answer questions quickly and efficiently without over answering the interrogatories and wasting time. If you simply do not understand an issue, do your best and move on. If you come across a subject or issue you've mastered, answer only what you need to and move on. The point is, by the time you get to the Bar you must *react* to what you see, there is very little time to think about or figure anything out.

Humility facilitates the absorption of new information. Why? Because the tame and submissive mind contains a burning desire to improve. You must see yourself continuously getting better and better in small increments as time passes. It is a helpful exercise to close your eyes and visualize yourself receiving new information, thanking the giver of that information and giving yourself an accommodation for receiving it in a spirit of humility. Your goal is to store the new information you have received in your subconscious, all the while filtering out any negativity you may perceive from their dissemination of criticism. With this method, you will find that when new challenges arise you have a vault of new skills and information to help you overcome that obstacle. Let's sum up what we have discussed regarding humility.

- Helps to interpret criticism
- Aids the learning process
- Creates a burning desire to learn
- Facilitates movement (to the next question)
- Helps to diagnose strengths and weaknesses

### Arrogance vs. Confidence

Some of us repeat takers are older. Older in the sense that we had full careers before going to law school. Many law school students are former accountants, police officers, private investigators, social workers, college professors, writers or media personalities, the list goes on and on. For your previous career you may have had to pass a licensing exam or draft a lengthy dissertation and justifiably these accomplishments have given you an air of self-confidence. The forthcoming caveat holds especially true for attorneys from other states who are taking the California Bar.

*Do not assume that the preparation you put into your prior licensing exam is sufficient to pass the California State Bar.* I'm one-hundred percent positive that each career I previously mentioned, among others, require the utmost preparation. And certainly you must use the skills you learned during your preparation to get ready for the test ahead. However, you cannot assume that because you were able to pass your prior licensing exam you will be able to pass this one with the same amount or less effort and time. Take this hypothetical example.

John graduated from law school in Texas. He was top of his class and paid three-thousand dollars for a top-notch Bar prep course. John studied hard, completed all his assignments and passed the Texas Bar on his first attempt. Fast forward 3 years and John discovers a great opportunity to practice worker's compensation law in California. He has a moderate case load in Texas yet doesn't have time for much else. In his haste to practice in California he assumes that since he is a lawyer in Texas he is required to take the California attorney's Bar to practice law there. He asks his secretary sign him up for the July Bar and figures he'll study for a month or so and "brush up" on criminal law. John is a fantastic civil attorney and knows civil procedure like the back of his hand so he doesn't feel the need to study civil law subjects. He also figures that since he is taking the attorney's Bar he does not have to study for the MBE.

His secretary tries to sign him up for the attorney's Bar but is told that John does not qualify (California requires that an applicant for the attorney Bar be in good standing in another jurisdiction for at least 4 years). The secretary figures the general Bar and attorney's Bar couldn't be that much different and John is a genius in her mind, therefore, he can pass either one. She signs him up for the general Bar.

It's May, and John lessens his case load. He settles some cases and consults fewer clients. He prepares by reading criminal law and procedure practice manuals, drafting criminal law motions, and takes timed essay questions over the weekends from the California Bar website. He cold calls a few criminal law attorneys in California to get their sense of the criminal law in their jurisdiction. John pays little attention to the civil subjects like Torts, Corporations, Community Property and Civil Procedure because he's been practicing law in those areas for over 3 years.

John gets his admittance card and sees that he is scheduled for the full 3-day general Bar. Confused he contacts the committee of Bar examiners who explain to him that he attempted to apply for the attorney's Bar but was denied admission due to insufficient time as a practicing lawyer in good standing in another jurisdiction. John contacts his secretary who explains what happened in full detail. John must either cancel his Bar admittance at a considerable fee or take the general exam unprepared.

What do you think John should do? No matter what you think John's best course of action is, the moral of the story is to see how John's arrogance has put him at a disadvantage no matter which route he chooses. If he takes the test, he's ill prepared for the MBE, the testable civil subjects and more importantly the physical and psychological, strain the Bar places on its examinees. If John forfeits and pays the fee, he has lost time, money from the clients he turned down to study, the cancellation fee and the opportunity to practice in California. Stop for a second and think of how John could have approached his opportunity to practice in California with more humility.

Let's use this same hypothetical and rework it so that John begins his journey humbly. John is a civil litigation attorney in Texas. He has been practicing for 3 full years. At happy hour after work a colleague tells John about making money as a worker's compensation attorney in California. John is looking to grow his practice and a change of scenery would be nice. He decides to apply to take the California State Bar.

John knows he is a great civil lawyer but realizes knows little about the California State Bar so he enrolls in a Bar-preparatory seminar in San-Francisco. He learns at the seminar that California tests state-law specific subjects including California evidence and civil procedure. He also learns that he must take the general Bar because he has not practiced law in Texas for the required time, therefore, he must prepare for the MBE also.

After careful consideration, John decides to put his plan to take the California Bar on hold until he meets the California Bar's jurisdictional practice time pre-requisite. In the interim, he reads essays, performance test questions and model answers from the California State Bar website all while still working his full case load. The time comes for John to sign up for the Bar. He applies to take the attorney's exam and is admitted. Three months before the exam John has significantly lightened his case load and is enrolled in a Bar prep course.

John has invested a lot of patience, time and effort into enrolling for the Bar. His mindset for preparing for the Bar is, "Just get it done." John promises to himself to put his ego aside and be amenable to being taught how to pass the Bar. During his prep course John, does not agree with how the tutor suggest he answer the essay questions. John understands certain nuances of civil procedure that could get these hypothetical clients greater money damages or orders for injunctions granted.  But, instead of trying to teach the class himself, John just focuses on answering the questions the way that the tutors are training him to.  After 3 months of practice John is confident that he is competent and well-prepared to pass the Bar.  John takes the test, passes and now has a multi-jurisdictional case load in Texas and California.

How does John's approach in the first hypothetical differ from the second?  In the first scenario, John was arrogant and made assumptions based on his arrogance.  He didn't feel the need to study civil subjects nor prepare for the MBE.  He was also comfortable delegating important duties to others without ensuring that they knew what they were doing.  Lastly, his arrogance cost him two valuable assets time and money.  *Don't let your past or even current achievements give you a false sense of security.*  Just because John is a successful civil attorney in Texas does not mean that he is not subject to the same pit-falls as a first-time Bar applicant in California.  If you are someone who has had success in your past career, it is your duty to distinguish whether the decision you make are motivated by arrogance or confidence.

## Can't teach an old dog new tricks?

Repeat takers come in all ages. I took the California State Bar between the ages of 28 through 32 years old. In my mind, I was supposed to have started practicing law by age thirty but it was two years past my deadline and I had yet to meet my goal. ARRGGHH! It so frustrated me back then. Now I understand that all that I needed would come in due time.

So how does this relate to practicing for the Bar? You may have concerns about whether you are amenable to learning new things because of your age. If so, you must replace that anxiety with a burning desire to master your craft. How do you do this? It's done by understanding that age is a partly a mindset. And anything that is within your perception is within your control.

For example, if you are in your late 40's or 50's you may have taken the Bar once or twice. Maybe you didn't pass and you have made the same mistakes that you made in your previous attempts. You figure that you can't teach an old dog new tricks and settle on taking it again one day. If this scenario describes you, know that you are on the verge of passing your exam. How so?

Firstly, you have proven that you have the intelligence to do legal analysis. You graduated from law school. Secondly, you have shown and proven perseverance because you are a repeat taker. This means that you have all the tools necessary to pass your exam. What you are missing is the right mind-set and approach to your preparation.

When you begin to prepare start with a humble disposition. Know that no matter your age, you can learn new things and should look forward to being challenged. You should expect to learn new things during your preparation. Be amenable to learning not only new law, but look to learn new things about your character. Are you testing the boundaries of your comfort zones? Try to learn new ways to practice, rest and approach confrontation.

With age comes maturity. Maturity should be perceived as an asset and not a hindrance. Mature people understand what is expected of them and use their experience as the backdrop to their preparation. As you begin to prepare for your next exam take some time to reflect on your past experiences with your exam.

Focus on the expectations of the exam and where you failed to meet those expectations. If you are unsure what the exam expects of you, then try to find out. I have a motto I like to live by, it says, "Try to find the answer to your questions yourself first, before you ask another person." Taking action this way is helpful in two ways. Firstly, doing your own investigation improves your research skills. And with enough practice you will be able to find information quickly which is invaluable as a sole practitioner or associate. We all understand that a professional's time is her number one asset and the ability to manage time efficiently goes a long way.

Secondly, finding out things yourself without the assistance of others leaves more opportunity for productive networking. Here's an example, suppose you have picked up a DUI case and need to find an expert on analyzing blood alcohol content (BAC) and the rising BAC defense. You could easily call a colleague and ask for a referral or you could do some internet research of your own, make a few calls and use your judgment as to your best choice. Using the second approach can now call your colleague prepared to engage in a dialogue about the merits of the experts in that field, instead of calling for a reference. Moreover, doing your own research before requesting the assistance of others, allows you to compare their referrals and suggestions to your own.

Do you find yourself writing more political or policy-based responses to the interrogatories? Writing opinion-based answers comes from your desire to be an advocate. If you have had a previous career or experienced some extraordinary event that was the catalyst for you becoming an attorney, then you may be a victim of over zealousness.  For the repeat takers who have a firm grasp on what area of law they plan to practice and issues they want to litigate, it is important to realize that the Bar or any professional licensing exam is not the place for you to express your political or social ideology.

For example, Judy, a recently divorced former school board administrator decides to go to law school and become an attorney.  Her passion for the profession came from seeing many children being pipelined through her city's educational system without proper representation.  With her knowledge of school board policies and procedures she felt that she would be a great advocate for children who were abused, neglected and mistreated by the school district personnel in her county.

Judy's painful and lengthy divorce fueled her determination.  During the dissolution proceedings Judy and her former husband, a savvy pitch man for a corporate marketing firm could not work together to come to a resolution.  Her husband wanted Judy to be responsible for marital debts he accrued without her knowledge during the marriage.  The court ordered Judy partially liable as the debts were community property.  This result angered Judy because she reasonably felt that she had been taken advantage of by her quick tongued ex-husband. Judy vowed that once she became an attorney, she would practice administrative and family law.

Fast forward 3 years and Judy is now sitting for her state's Bar. She opens the first page of her exam and see a torts questions with a fact pattern involving a young girl who skips school to make some money washing cars at a gas station near the school site. Ultimately the young girl is injured, and her parents call an attorney to sue the school for allowing their daughter to be harmed while under the school's supervision.

After the first read Judy cannot believe that this type of question has appeared on her Bar exam. Before she starts to outline Judy remembers talking to her Bar exam tutor who constantly reminded her to stay within in the confines of the question and to not get side tracked. Judy then constructs a perfect outline to follow for her essay, consisting of only the most relevant issues in the hypothetical. About half way through the essay Judy decides to apply some administrative law codes she remembers from her years as a school board employee. In her mind, Judy knows that the Bar graders will be very impressed with the depth of her knowledge regarding a school district's duty to keep students on the campus grounds. After writing each paragraph Judy carefully reviews each phrase to ensure that her argument follows a perfect

I.R.A.C format and ends in a well-reasoned and logical conclusion.

After about 50 minutes of writing Judy realizes that she could end this essay and move on to the next. But, she has 10 more minutes to write. Judy, then decides to add one more paragraph expressing societal concerns regarding truancy and the public policy implications of allowing the school district to go unpunished if the court were to hold in its favor. Judy writes for 30 minutes instead of 10. Once she realizes that she has expended too much time on this one essay she hurries to bring it to an end so she can review the next question. To Judy's surprise it is a community property question about a young couple getting divorced and the distribution of community property debts.

I'll stop here. What problem does Judy face at this moment? She has already gone over time on her first essay. Granted it was a subject she felt passionate about, but now she must answer another question that also excites the advocate in her. Does she cut the second essay short? Should she not be concerned with the time and answer the question as thoroughly as possible? Should she skip ahead to the 3$^{rd}$ question, answer it quickly as possible, then return to the community property question? All of the choices are arguably justifiable. However, it's irrelevant what Judy does at this point. The lesson here is to not put yourself in the position to have to decide. Obviously, Judy should have stopped with a 10-minute surplus and omitted her public policy rant. The key here is to understand that your licensing exam is not the place for you to step out as an advocate for a cause or issue. Save that energy for when you are a licensed practicing attorney.

### Changing natural and/or learned reactions.

Now that you have tuned your mind toward humility let's focus on understanding the value of practice. We can change our natural and learned reactions to certain unfamiliar contexts through practice. Generally, when we encounter something new we rely on our past experiences to aid us in completing the task. Our brain uses prior experiences as a context to influence how we ultimately react to a new challenge. Sometimes, our experience is not enough to rely on alone, therefore, we need to train our minds and bodies to react in the appropriate manner to succeed.

The Bar tests, in part, how we react to unfamiliar contexts. First is problem solving. Here, you are called upon to spot and solve multiple issues through legal analysis. Second, is reacting to life's little hiccups or the unforeseeable events that occur when taking a lengthy exam. For example, if you encounter an algebra equation such as: $x + 1 = 4$ and you have never solved an equation such as this you may rely on your experience with algebra or use fundamental mathematical principles to help you get through it. The same reaction will occur when you come across a question on the Bar that you are unfamiliar with. The good thing about legal analysis is there is no one correct answer as opposed to my simple algebraic equation.

Your Bar grader is looking for a thorough analysis based on the application of fact to law stated in a lawyer-like manner. No matter what question you encounter your reaction to it must be the same. First, apply the facts to the law that you have memorized. Then state exactly why this fact satisfies or fails to satisfy an element of law and finally state your conclusion. Fundamentally, it's really that simple.

You might be asking, "What if I encounter an issue that calls for a rule of law I simply do not remember?" My suggestion is to rely on your experience to guide you to a common-sense rule. After all, laws are created to promote order, predictability and fairness. You will be surprised how much Legislative intent we have ingrained in us through American culture. If you spot an issue that calls for a rule you cannot remember simply think of a familiar story that contains a similar context.

For example, I had the hardest time with Corporations essays when practicing for the Bar exam. I did not take business associations as an elective in law school and I had no personal interest or experience in the subject. Or did I? When I got a Corporations essay on one of my practice exams, I could remember freezing up because it all seemed so foreign and based on very specific rules that only made sense in the corporate world.

One practice question concerned trading stock with 10b-5 insider trading liability as a main issue. If you don't know the elements of this cause of action don't worry because at the time neither did I. But I sat for a moment and thought about what I did know about corporations and stock trading and it came to me. Ah ha! Trading Places, a movie starring Eddie Murphy and Dan Aykroyd. I simply loved this movie growing up and I used it as a backdrop to help understand my corporations essay. I just imagined the characters in the essay as the actors from the movie. The movie's plot centered around the Dukes (two wealthy brothers who owned a commodities brokerage firm). They planned to corner the orange juice market by getting their hands on a confidential crop report days before the information was to go public. Their plan was to use their inside knowledge to leverage the stock price for oranges on a particular trading day.

The practice essay was similar in that someone had inside knowledge that was used to gain an unlawful profit based on a stock trade. To help calm my nerves and get a sense of where to start, I asked myself how would this essay turn out if the parties had the same disposition as the characters the movie? Thinking about the essay in those terms opened my imagination and allowed me to create a common-sense rule of law for 10b-5. Often, all you need is a catalyst to jump start your imagination. Creating an analogy from something fun and familiar can put you at ease. When you are at ease, your analytical creativity can flow naturally from your interpretation of the fact pattern.

Next time you come across a subject you are uncomfortable with try to *relate it to a story, movie, song or context that you are familiar with*. Generally, you will not find a perfect match but that's not your goal. The point is to put yourself in a state of mind where you are amenable to combining the power of your imagination and the depth of your life experience to create rules of law that are applicable to the issues you have spotted.

## Administration: Reacting to Foreseeable and Unforeseeable Events

When preparing for any licensing exam you must evaluate all the foreseeable mishaps that may occur. Create an informal checklist. Make sure to you mark off certain tasks to be completed before the exam. The list does not have to be exhaustive, however, it must contain the common obstacles that come up during a lengthy exam.

For example, your check list must include a supply list. The night before your exam make sure you have pencils, erasers, pens, scratch paper, power cord to your laptop, a timer/clock etc. You may be thinking that everyone knows to bring these supplies, but, I can tell you from personal experience that many students forget to bring the most mundane items. These simple supplies can have a substantial impact on your ability to be calm during the exam. Imagine having five minutes to start your multiple-choice exam and you only have one pencil or even worse – NONE AT ALL! You can ask your neighbor or a friendly face, but the panic accompanied with scrounging around for a pencil will carry over into the exam itself.

You only have one pencil and decide that you can make it through the exam with just that one. Assume Murphy's Law kicks in and SNAP the pencil breaks. Now you must overcome your initial shock, find another pencil, gather yourself and continue the exam all the while losing precious time and increasing your anxiety. Here's a quick story.

During one of my Bar exams, I did not have all my supplies. It's the second day of the exam (the MBE) and I reach into my Ziploc bag only to realize I had one pencil. It was a big red elementary school style pencil (probably one of my kid's pencils) with barely any lead left. I took one look at it and was utterly disappointed in myself. I studied so much and practiced for months only to overlook something as simple as having a fresh pencil. Luckily, I knew one of the students down the row and asked to borrow one of hers. Now, I survived that MBE administration, but, not without some embarrassment from having to ask someone for a pencil.

At first glance, my story may invoke a feeling of disbelief. However, I can assure you over-looking the pencil had very little to do with my work ethic at the time. An oversight like the one just mentioned is not for lack of overall effort, it's caused by the extreme pressure like an entrance exam puts on an applicant.

Undoubtedly, licensing exams are highly competitive. Even the slightest sign of incompetence and/or unpreparedness can create an unbearable feeling of inadequacy. Your test-mates will pick up on it like blood in the water to hungry sharks. Not to say that having to borrow a pencil will derail your whole exam. But, why chance it? *Create a simple check list and mark off your necessary supplies the night before the exam.*

Another foreseeable calamity to avoid is disorientation and hurriedness due to unfamiliarity with your environment. Generally, licensing exams are administered in downtown areas in major cities where the hustle and bustle can be intimidating if you are unfamiliar with the surroundings. *Be sure to visit the test site before the exam.* When visiting the site locate the exits and entrances to the site, view the testing area if possible. It's helpful to walk around the block and surrounding areas. When touring, look for restaurants you may like for lunch during the exam. Look for coffee shops if you like to have caffeine in the morning. You can never be sure how the morning or afternoon of an exam will unfold, so it's best to be familiar with your environment so that you can react quickly in case you are late but need a quick coffee.

More importantly, visiting the test site gives you the opportunity to use your imagination. As you walk the site and surrounding areas, take a few moments to visualize yourself on exam day. See yourself herding into the building with hundreds of other students. Listen for the clamor of gossip and see yourself ignoring it. Next, pretend it's the morning time. Is it cold (did you bring a jacket)? Are you starving? Where is the coffee shop? Do you recognize anyone? How will you react to them wanting to talk to you right before, after or even during the exam?

Now, imagine it's the afternoon and you are poised to find a deli or pizza place to eat lunch. See yourself paying for your lunch. Are you using cash or a debit card? Do you recognize anyone in there? Are they talking about the exam? Will you join in the conversation or be a loner? Performing a mental dress rehearsal gives your brain a context to rely on when an unfamiliar situation or split-second decision needs to be made.

For lunch, try and eat a small but healthy lunch. Why? Because you don't want the super burrito you ate to come back and haunt you during the exam. I can remember seeing tens of students leave the exam to go to the bathroom only to lose 5 to 10 minutes of precious exam time. Do yourself a favor and purchase a chicken salad with soup or a sandwich. The 5-item bento box with a side of tempura shrimp may look delicious but you don't want to either have to go to the bathroom or suffer through chronic sleepiness brought on by having to digest a huge lunch.

Now you have made it on time. You have your morning coffee, you know where your lunch spot is located, and you ordered moderately. You ate just enough to hold you over until the end of the exam. GREAT! Let's switch gears and focus on another foreseeable reality that WILL ABSOLUTELY OCCUR no matter how prepared you are or what test you are taking. That being, not knowing some of the substantive material being tested.

There will be an issue, rule or context tested on the exam that you have not encountered. More likely you, will have encountered it, but not proficient enough with the subject matter to be able to analyze it competently at first glance. The rule for this inevitability is to first understand that it will happen. The examiners scour the law looking for issues that students either traditionally have trouble with or avoid, like issues that require factual familiarity or memorizing a mathematical formula for example. You may encounter subject matter based on an elective that you have not taken.

When you encounter something on the test that you either have not seen or are unfamiliar with follow these steps. First, take few seconds to breath and realize that even if you have not memorized the substantive material required to analyze this question, YOU CAN STILL PASS THE EXAM!

Now, read the question and use your memory to place the fact pattern in a familiar context. Next create a simple outline or framework to build upon, one common analytical legal framework is IRAC or Issue, Rule, Analysis, Conclusion. Write those headings out and use them as guide posts. Next, (if you don't know the rule) create a rule that appeals to common sense. Analyze by arguing whether the facts satisfy the elements of law you have created in your rule. Make sure to use all the facts and draw a conclusion. And finally, the hardest part - MOVE ON!

The ability to show competence in the face of challenging work is difficult, but it's not enough. You must learn to trust your strategy and the only way to earn trust in any strategy is to use it and see it work in real time. Take the two questions, putting the most difficult question last. Start with question one and begin to solve. Once you are done with question one move on to question two. You know that question two is the difficult subject so it's no surprise. Then implement your strategy for solving problems you are unfamiliar with.

Once you have finished question two, take a short pause (1 minute). Take all the frustration, anxiety, shame, regret and any other negative feelings that were conjured up during the question and let it go. "How do I let it go" you may ask?

Tell yourself this, "I expected this would happen, I stayed with my strategy, even if this answer is incorrect, I can still pass, I must move on." Please be creative and come up with your own mantra to reassure yourself that no matter how badly you may perform on one question there are still points to be earned throughout the remainder of the exam.

CAVEAT, if you find yourself repeating this mantra during the test for multiple questions, then understand that you have not memorized enough substantive material, and/or you have not exposed yourself to the requisite number of testable contexts. In the world of test taking there are many foreseeable obstacles that may occur, many of which I have not mentioned here. Right here, right now get a sheet of paper.

----- Go ahead, I'll wait for you-----

Brainstorm any number of things that you can think of that can throw a wrench into your plan to pass your next exam. When you are done, put the paper in a folder near your study materials and save it for your last week of review. During that last week pull it out to refresh your memory on mistakes you can avoid. As a warning, remember that you don't want to harp on the negative. So, do not obsess with what could go wrong. The sheet of paper is just a reminder of things that tend to slip by us when taking a test.  Keep it, look at it and move on.

What about the unforeseeable events, how can we prepare for those?  To prepare for things we don't expect to happen is to practice controlling our panic response.  Generally, with a calm mind most unforeseeable issues can be resolved.  It's when we panic does the unforeseeable have a dramatic effect on our performance.

For example, during my final attempt at the Bar the power went out, disabling about a third of the student's laptops.  Luckily my section was not affected, however, there was much clamor and panic swirling about.  Many students began to unplug their laptops in search of a working power strip, others resolved to just handwrite their exams.  Some just sat there and expected the proctors to solve the issue.  Easier to come up with an answer while reading this book, rather than during the exam.  It's almost impossible not to feel some uneasiness when something like that occurs.  What would you have done?

The best thing to do in this situation is to be calm.  Realize that if something unforeseeable occurs (not of your own doing) that totally prevents you from finishing the exam the examiners likely have some remedy for you.  However, where an unlikely event causes a delay or some discomfort, your job is to not allow it to knock you off your goal, that being, to display competence throughout the exam. In our example of the power going out, you may want to decide quickly that you want to hand write your answers. What if your handwriting is terrible? Then quickly get to a working power-strip. The key is to not waste time pouting, giving up or questioning why this has happened to you. If the proctors have indicated that the test will resume despite the mishap, then understand that you can overcome it and still pass.

What about sickness? It's a few days before your exam and you have studied like crazy. But you forgot to care for your health (not sleeping) and you feel a cold coming on or severe fatigue setting in. Aside from being diagnosed with a terminal illness a doctor's note will not get you out of the exam. You are going to have to take the exam while fighting your cold. The best course is to take precautionary measures and be healthy throughout your preparation. If you still get sick, then bring to the test, non-drowsy medications, a pillow for comfort and get plenty of rest the day before.

# Perfect Practice Makes Perfect

A successful athlete understands good practice habits. As a test taker, you must also come to this understanding. In this section, I'll discuss some the virtues associated with productive practice and habitual visualization while using law of attraction.

When a process is repeated, be it physical or mental the brain creates a context and stores it as a memory. Neuropathways are reinforced when a person repeats a process over and over. This is how we become proficient at rote tasks. If you are an athlete or know one you probably can relate to what I've just explained.

Like how an athlete must first learn the fundamentals of a skill before he or she can be proficient at more advanced maneuvers, you must practice the fundamentals of legal analysis before attempting to answer questions under time pressure.

One of the most important tools a Bar exam taker must have is the ability to outline their thoughts before attempting to write the exam. It is crucial that you allocate time in your study schedule to learn how to outline and for practicing the outlining technique you have chosen to use.

Step 1: Take out a practice essay and outline (only) one issue that you have spotted. Next review the model answer and see how your outline stacks up to the analysis in the model answer for that issue. If your outline is missing some key analysis go back and fill in the missing parts into your outline. This should take no more than 30 minutes.

Step 2: REST about 10 to 15 mins

Step 3: Take out a completely different practice essay outline one issue that you have spotted. Next review the model answer and see how your outline compares to the analysis in the model answer for that issue. If your outline is missing key analyses, go back and fill in the missing parts to your outline. This should take no more than 30 minutes.

Step 4: REST about 10 to 15 mins

Step 5: Without review go back re-read the 1st practice essay and outline the same issue again. Then compare that outline with the updated outline from your first go-round. Is your outline comparable to your updated outline?

Step 6: Without review go back re-read the 2nd practice essay and outline the same issue again. Then compare your 2nd outline with the updated outline from your first go-round. Is your outline comparable to your updated outline?

But Curtis, what if my outlining is fine I just missed a related issue, or I didn't know a rule of law or exception. This means that you have not memorized enough substantive law. You must know each element necessary to prove up an issue. If this describes you, go back into your substantive materials and simplify the rule of law and its component elements in a way that you can remember. Creating *Mnemonics* are a great way to memorize the elements of law.

Another great way to fish out elements or rules of law are to scrutinize the facts of the hypothetical. Think of it this way, if there is a fact there is an issue or element to apply it to. I can recall taking an essay writing seminar in law school and the professor had a mantra, "From the FACTS the ISSUES arise." It simply does not work the other way around.

The point of this exercise is that it's more productive to practice simple tasks in short time frames with periods of rest rather than attempting marathon practice sessions. In our example, we started off with something easy like spotting one issue and outlining that one issue only. Then we checked our analysis with that of the model answer. Next, we switched to a completely new essay and repeated the process. Skipping to another essay allows the brain to "forget" what you just corrected. Then we come back to the original essay without review and see if we have retained what we learned from comparing our first outline with the analysis in the model answer.

How does this relate to the value of repetition? What we are doing besides working on our outlining and analytical skills is repeating the process of outlining itself. First, we do it cold with no model to draw from. Then we fill-in the gaps with the analysis from the model answer. We do this process with another essay then REPEAT the process but with the memory of the model analysis in mind. With this formula, we have written 4 outlines in 1 hour! Two of the outlines are likely deficient and our brain remembers the corrections and mistakes we made when compared to the model answer. The other two outlines should be improved, and the brain will remember what it feels like to draft a more complete and accurate outline. Which experience do you think your brain will draw from under time pressure during the exam? Right! The experience with the best result.

How do I know if what I'm doing is counter-productive? After doing your practice are you seeing positive results?  Notice I said positive results.  If the answer is NO.  Then it's either how (technique) or what (substance) you are practicing that is not right.  If your scores are remaining the same, then your practice regime must be modified.  Correct practice always produces positive results.  In short, practicing just for the sake of practicing will NOT produce the skills necessary to show competence on the exam.

**The Law of Attraction: Visualizing Your Results**

The law of attraction is just that. A LAW! So, the Universe must obey it.  If you have never heard of the law of attraction, take a moment and type in, "law of attraction" or "The Secret" into google or your web-browser of choice.  The law of attraction is universal.  It states, "what you think about comes about, whether it be negative or positive."  Translate this command into practice and visualize success. Through this practice success is more likely to occur. It's highly beneficial to visualize and see yourself practicing and producing positive results.

For example, the night before you are set to practice, visualize yourself sitting quietly practicing.  See yourself thinking and using the tools your instructor has suggested, the tools you have thought of as well as the tools you have picked up from this book and other supplemental materials. Now see yourself having some difficulty with a problem. See yourself not being discouraged. See yourself cross checking, editing and reviewing your answers. Next, see yourself taking on another problem and applying the knowledge you have learned from your review. Finally see the increased score and relish in the feeling of accomplishment and the fact that you CAN and WILL improve with proper training.

Do this every night. Do an abbreviated version of this visualization exercise five or ten minutes before you start practicing each time. Eventually, doing this will become natural, you will do it without even thinking about it, it will be second nature and you will start thinking of your potential in only positive terms.

To some this may sound like a bunch of hocus pocus, to others it will resonate either because they have tried it before or it will just make sense. What this positive visualization exercise will do is give your brain a context, one where you are successful. Your mind will subliminally recall this exercise when scanning for a way to produce positive results. Your imagination is very powerful. There is neuroscientific evidence that the brain does not distinguish between what is real and what is imagined.

You might be saying, "Well I've tried that before and it doesn't work." But - did you also imagine flaws and struggles? Or just the success. You must do BOTH. There will be obstacles. There will be challenges. There will be issues you don't spot and rules of law you don't remember every element to. Therefore, give your brain a "realistic" vision of what is to come. The important part of the exercise is to visualize yourself going through the process of correcting your mistakes, then seeing the results you desire because of your review and practice.

The visualization exercise is very important during the week or so before your exam. You want to give your mind as much positive context to draw from. Visualize yourself sitting for the entire exam. See yourself starting off strong and feeling confident. See yourself executing your strategy for choosing which question to answer first. See yourself being very familiar with most of the material. See yourself checking the time consistently and confidently. See yourself coming across a problem that you aren't so familiar with. Do you panic? NO. See yourself taking a breath, relating that problem to something you are familiar with. Answer it as best you can. Be satisfied with your answer and MOVE ON!

Continue to visualize until you get to the end of the exam. You are feeling good, you felt like you gave 100 percent and for most of the test you felt confident and more importantly

COMPETENT. Yes, a FEW of the problems were tricky but for the most part you nailed it. Now see yourself going on with life after the exam. You have a natural anxiety about your score but you aren't overly nervous nor are you cocky or arrogantly believing you have passed for sure. You just know that you gave your preparation and your execution 100 percent. Finally, see the day where you check your e-mail or receive a letter from the committee who administers the test. Open it. What does it say? Now open your eyes.

You have officially created a reality in your mind that you have already passed your exam. Your subconscious mind (with repeated uses of this exercise) will begin to adjust and make decisions that will lead to your ultimate success.

Let me tell you a quick story. I struggled with the Bar for many years. During those years I spoke to some of my colleagues and mentors about other opportunities and other ventures I could pursue. One person stands out in my mind. And he gave his opinion of me. He said, "Curtis, no matter what you do, I believe that ultimately you will be successful." It is my opinion that he saw in me, in my drive, that I had resolved to succeed. At the time, he was someone I admired and respected, so I held his opinion in the highest regard. I figured that if he could see that I would ultimately succeed then I would.

This same theory applies to you. Make up in your mind that you will succeed no matter what and part of that process starts with creating a mental virtual reality where you have experienced success. What positive things have people told you about yourself? Believe it. Because it's true. You must keep adjusting, keep learning and refining your vision.

The law of attraction takes time to work. There will be times when you forget to do the exercise, then something will remind you to do it. Don't feel discouraged when this happens (notice I said when and not if). But do not fret, there are tools to help you remember. Try creating a vision board. Take a poster board of whatever size and write mantras, cut out pictures from magazines, books or google image searches and place them on the board. Hang it up somewhere you will see it often.

I didn't use a vision-board during the Bar, but fortunately my wife reminded me of the concept after we'd moved from the California bay area back to Sacramento. She'd researched the law of attraction after I passed the Bar and reminded me of this tool. We immediately created one and hung it up in our bedroom. Sometimes I stand in front of it and visualize the images coming to life. More importantly I visualize what work I need to do to obtain those things. Most of the time though I catch a glimpse of it while just being in the room, paying no conscious attention to it. However, I know it's in my peripheral, thus, I'm reminded of its contents every day without even trying.

Another way to ensure you practice this technique is to calendar a visualization session using Microsoft outlook or other calendaring software. Set your reminder to reoccur and every time you get a notice - stop what you are doing and start imagining. You will be surprised at how effective it is for preparing for exams and the other dreams in life you certainly have.

The vision-board works. I know from experience. After compiling the images from our board, the images within a few months became our reality. You may be thinking, "Curtis, you just purchased those items because you see them every day. That may well be true for somethings but certainly not for others. For example, I had a client who wanted to pay me for legal services with a puppy. He told me his dog had a new litter and in addition to money he'd supplement my compensation with a dog. I said, "Ok." Besides, my kids and I wanted a dog. Shortly thereafter, my wife and I created the vision board and on it was a dog. It was a brown and white pit bull of some breed. I wasn't particularly fond of pit bulls and my father even advised against getting one. But we randomly found a picture in a magazine and it was a regal looking k9 so we used the image for our board.

Months passed and the timing never seemed right for my family to have a dog until one day, he called me. I came to his home and he delivered to me a brown pit bull with a white belly. Now, when I look at the board and then I look at our family dog. I feel that I played a role in attracting this dog to my family. Other material items like furniture, trips, habits etc.... have also sprung from the board into reality. I cannot be sure if it's magic or something I'm doing and frankly I don't really care. All I know is that once the board was up, the things on it started becoming reality. Now here is the kicker; a mock-up of the cover of this book is on our vision board, so... if you are reading this, then guess what?

**Consistent Practice is Key**

Whenever I come across a situation where I feel unprepared or my knowledge base is not where I like it to be, I like to say it's because I'm not swimming in it. What that means is I'm not surrounded by the material such that I feel like it's all around me, like when swimming in water. For your exam, you must be swimming in contexts. Notice I did not say substantive material. No. You must be exposing yourself to the material in various contexts as much as you possibly can.

This includes but not limited to:

1. Talking with colleagues about the material.
2. Doing practice exams.
3. Watching TV shows related to your subject.
4. Reading print media related to your subject.
5. Being personally present with others and talking about your subject.
6. Engaging in friendly competition related to your subject.
7. NOW YOU THINK OF ONE.

To get to a place where you are swimming in the material/contexts you must get value out of every second of every day until the end of the exam. A great way to start on this path is to have a practice set of multiple choice questions in the bathroom. Now, every time you sit down to use the bathroom you are squeezing value out of every minute of every day. (It's ok to laugh.) Also, some of us have free time when we don't realize it. Taking the kids to the park? Bring along some practice questions. Taking the kids to karate/basketball/baseball or ballet? Bring along some practice questions. On a long trip? Take recordings of lectures/outlines/practice questions.

This method rings true especially during the last few weeks before the exam. Try to expose yourself to the material from different perspectives and angles for as much time as you can by integrating it into your everyday life. In short, you must expose yourself to the material during "other" times that are not specifically allocated to studying.

**Translating Practice into Execution**

Michael Jordan said it best, "I practice just like I'm in an actual game so when I'm playing I already know what I'm capable of." If there is anything that you must remember from this book it's this, practice best translates into useable execution in real-time when you practice in context. This is an explanation of passive versus active learning. With passive learning, we are simply absorbing the information through our senses. Active learning allows absorption through using information that we have passively learned. Therefore, in-order to actively learn with minimal frustration, we must first passively observe the material. While doing thousands of multiple choice questions and tens of essays will certainly sharpen your skills, nothing ensures results like practicing in a context like the real exam.

You must be ready to practice in exam like conditions otherwise your practice time will not be used optimally. For example, it's counterproductive to sit for a full practice Bar exam if you are not familiar with test nor have a gauge of what your strengths and weaknesses are. Therefore, you must first learn the fundamentals, then practice basic analysis with no pressure. Once you have a base then set up practice scenarios that simulate actual test conditions and execute. Here is a quick run-down. First, read up on a subject. Then try several questions of varying difficulty. Now sit for an entire timed session based on the parameters of your exam. Grade your score. Edit and review your thought process and analysis. Take another timed session. This process must be applied to the entire exam as well. Finally, sit for an entire practice exam under time conditions near the time right before you take the actual test.

Here is a list of suggestions for effective practice:

1. Study the subject then practice your technique for mastering that subject.
2. Rest when you get tired.
3. Most of your practicing should be done ALONE. Although group sessions are useful, keep them to a minimum.

4. Practice consistently. It is more effective to practice 5 days for 2 hours rather than 2 days for 10 hours.
5. Track your progress.
6. Look for bad technique (notice I didn't say results) and remedy.
7. Practice at different locations and different times. (Not just at the library from 10am to 8pm)

**Time Management Basics**

You can't learn it all at once. You can't become competent all at once and you certainly can't master it all at once. Your exam will require a consistent, steady, regimented and prolonged practice schedule to show competence. This will require you to augment and change your study schedule as your practice reveals your strengths and weaknesses.

Distinguish what you want to do verses what you should be doing. If you like doing multiple choice in one subject area and you get high scores you shouldn't spend the bulk of your practice time doing multiple choice in that area. This sounds simple, but many test takers fool themselves into believing that they can score 100% in a certain section, thus making up for shortcomings in another.

Most of the time what you should be doing are the activities that cause you some discomfort or make you nervous. If you cannot analyze an issue, then break it down into its smallest parts and work each part independently until you are comfortable with the entire process. For many of us this would be *outlining* your analysis before attempting the answer the question. This applies to multiple choice as well as fill in the blank and essay questions. If you forget to outline, or outline insufficiently then you know where to start. Begin with the basics, research various outlining formats and find one that resonates with you. It does not have to be complicated, but it must be effective. Learn what your weaknesses are. Break down the analytical skill required and spend your time practicing that.

So, you have finished practicing one technique and it's time to switch it up to give your brain an opportunity to develop another skill. This interim is called a "transition." There are soft transitions and hard transitions and benefits and detriments to both. Soft transitions are an extended pause. It's a rest period where you either shut down (rest) for however long and come back to your study/preparation OR do something completely unrelated to your practice. Soft transitions are beneficial because it allows you to recharge, refuel and just get away from the pressure of learning a new technique. Soft transitions also aid in avoiding burnout. They are detrimental in that one must be diligent to avoid turning a soft transition into abandonment or complete loss of momentum. For example, you do 100 multiple choice questions (1 hour) and decide to soft transition into the grading and review portion of your study. You decide to grab a bite to eat and lay down. Suddenly you wake up and 45 minutes to an hour has passed. At this point you must wake yourself back up, sharpen your focus and get back to grading your multiple choice. Here, the transition has cost you time and momentum. Instead, stay where you are, set your timer for 10 minutes close your eyes. When the timer goes off start to grade and review.

Hard transitions occur when you switch from one task to another without a break. Hard transitions are beneficial because you get a strong sense of accomplishment when you go directly from one task to the next. Your focus stays sharp (so long as you don't burnout) and often your focus will increase with hard transitions. Also, they are a great time saver and confidence builder.

Hard transitions are detrimental because burnout is inevitable if you do not calculate how long the next task will take. Your ability to retain information drops after a certain point, so be cognizant of your attention span. (Are you just reading the words or are you engaged in the problem-solving process?) In our prior example, it took only 1 hour to complete one set of multiple-choice questions. However, it may take two or even three times that long for the grading and review. If you hard transition directly into grading and review at some point your focus will wane. Therefore, to have a productive review process, you must transition into it properly. In this case a soft transition would be optimal.

The best way to make effective use of your time is to implement both soft and hard transitions. You can set up a pattern of transitions based on practice timeline.

For example:

Task A (Soft Transition)
Task B (Soft Transition)
Task C (Hard Transition)
Task D (Soft Transition)
Task E (Hard Transition)
Task D (Finished)

The key is you determine how long your soft transitions are and at what times you need to hard transition depending on your abilities. Remember that studying/practicing when you are burned out or unable to retain the information or technique is counter-productive and will hurt you far more than the time you lose stopping to rest.

Knowing when to stop for the day is also key. Try to schedule out your study session so you have a definite end time. We attempt to micro manage our time but it's hard to follow it perfectly every day. Why? Because life is organic. Often other responsibilities take precedent over our study schedule because things come up that need to be taken care of. Don't fight it. Practice being calm when something unexpected takes you away from your study time. Use your discretion when deciding how much time, if any, you will devote to addressing unexpected interruptions.

This idea can be summed up in what's called the Mañana doctrine. This maxim can be stated simply as, "don't do today what will take care of itself tomorrow." For example, you may feel very energetic after a long day of studying so you decide to go for an extra hour or two for good measure. You take on another section that you had scheduled for tomorrow. On the surface, this may seem like a good idea, but if you have planned it for tomorrow, do it then. Staying on schedule is also a skill we must practice even when it appears that going ahead is beneficial. You want to leave your study session hungry for more, not burned out and frustrated.

## Staying Motivated

I took the Bar five times and over the years I've learned to be proud of it. I discovered that not only did I earn the grand prize (being licensed to practice law) but I also picked up a host of new skills because of my perseverance. One of the skills that I learned during that time was the ability to keep myself motivated toward achieving my goals.

Being highly motivated over a long course of study is nearly impossible. Eventually monotony and the effect of the daily grind wears you down until you lose the energy it takes to get up and study your hardest. Remember the path to success is a journey and your motivation will rise and fall. But there are some techniques you can use to revive your motivation once it fades.

Leave your study sessions hungry for more. We talked about this briefly in the last section. It's good practice to put your study to rest at a moment when you are still anxious to learn more. This often happens when you have picked up a new technique and are excited to use it. This fervor will carry over into the next session when it's time to begin studying the next day. With this technique, you will experience less resistance when getting back to studying the next day.

Develop your ability to convert negative energy into drive. Failure causes us to get down on ourselves, failure also heightens our insecurities. However, those feelings can be converted into drive. This drive motivates you to keep going. You can do this by changing your response to failure and interpreting it from another perspective.

Start by redefining your definition of failure. See failure as an opportunity, see it as a signal. Do not view failure as a set-back or shortcoming. Incorrect answers, faulty analysis, not finishing before the timer goes off, these things contain the gems to your ultimate success. True and pure failure occurs only when you choose to give up. So long as you are trying to improve you have not failed.

When you don't get the results you want (the common perception of failure) you remain where you were before attempting the challenge. Simply put, in no way have you digressed or gone backward. Actually, you have move forward. How? From failure comes more information. Information about what is needed to progress. Before you try and don't succeed you don't know what needs to be improved for you to level up.

Sounds simple, right? It's easily said but more difficult in practice. Focus on the feeling you get after discovering a faulty technique, finding the correct way to execute it, doing it the right way and finally getting the results, you deserve! Without the process of not getting instant positive results (i.e. failure) you cannot appreciate this feeling.

## THE LAST DAYS TIPS AND TRICKS

Month one

The beginning is a good time to refresh your recollection of the substantive law. *Filling in flow charts* are a good way to revive your memory of those 1L and 2L core subjects that you haven't studied for a while. Flow charts are great for recognizing exceptions to general rules, distinctions between state, federal and model codes and the analytical frameworks necessary to solve element based issues. (e.g. civil procedure: personal jurisdiction). You can purchase flow charts from a law school book store or online. I recommend you use flow charts.

*Reading cases* to break up the monotony of filling in flow charts is a great way to learn the law in context while preventing burnout and frustration. Read the cases casually, now is the time to read case law fact patterns for leisurely purposes. Here, you are interjecting a change of pace to keep from getting bored with flow charts. Also, the examiners sometimes take fact patterns from actual cases and use them as templates to create test questions. Taking abbreviated notes is ok.

Outlining is *not* recommended. Detailed legal outlining was a new and challenging task in law school, but that time is over and not useful in preparing for the Bar. Do not outline.

### Months two and three

During last two months practice multiple choice questions, essays and performance tests. Your practice will require some review of the law. Make sure you have a study schedule to keep you on course toward competence. Remember, studying for the Bar or any licensing exam is not a complete overhaul of your substantive knowledge and analytical technique. Your goal is to find those fine line areas that need to be improved. *It's going to be small adjustments that improve your Issue spotting, organization and analytical skills that get you to a level of competence.*

Do not attempt to "redo law school" to make up for feeling guilty for not getting straight As. Do not attempt to memorize every nuance of law by outlining every subject in perfect detail. Your goal is to find the subject matter that needs refreshing. To do so will require exposure to the hundreds of contexts that legal issues are tested in. The examiners have traditional modes and contexts in which they test legal issues. Over time you will be able to easily spot the, common testable issues the examiners what you to know.

## The week before the exam

Around three days before your exam rest, be calm and put the preparation behind you. You want to be sober and begin to *envision the immediate future.* On exam-day your mind will play tricks on you. After completing a section, you may be tempted to predict how you did. Doing this is a waste of time, it will only distract you from finishing strong. The key is to do your best and move on. If you notice an obvious miscue, remind yourself that you can make up for it with a stronger effort on the next section. I experienced this after finishing the essays right before taking the last performance test. It was the last day of the exam and after I completed essay number six I realized during lunch that I didn't spot an issue on equitable remedies.

I can remember being so down on myself for not spotting what I thought was an obvious issue. I thought that mistake had ruined my chances of passing. I sulked during lunch time and on into the exam hall. Then literally right before I started the performance test, something came over me. I realized that I had an opportunity to make up for it. The cause of the realization was having faced adversity during my study and overcoming it. I could recall from past practice tests feeling badly about a section but finishing strong and achieving a passing score.

I realized that the performance test counted for a higher percentage of points than one issue on one exam. Once I understood what I needed to do my entire attitude changed. I went into that performance test determined to *finish strong*. And I did, I remember leaving that exam confident. I was sure in my performance because I knew I exhibited competence throughout. I resisted the urge to get everything right and focused on being consistently competent and finishing strong.

# The Groundhog Day Effect

I took the California State Bar five times.
And at one point, it felt like I was stuck in a time
loop. The same pattern kept repeating. I'd study,
take the Bar, not pass, then look for a job - repeat.
During my third and fourth attempts, my wife got
pregnant twice around the same time I would take
the Bar. For two years in a row, I'd take the Bar
and then we would have a baby.

Being caught in a loop is no fun. You start to
see and hear the same things. You can literally
feel the inertia of failure pushing against your
will to move on. You talk to people about it, but
like lobotomized zombies they just keep
suggesting the same things, like study more, take
a break, pay for a class, think about doing
something else besides law etc. None of it really
helps and the harder you try the more frustrating
it can become.

For me, recognizing and ultimately breaking
this pattern was tough but going through the
process made me understand that I had to change
something about myself before I could move
forward. I realized that to grow I had to change
myself. This was about more than just my study
habits it was also about becoming a *better person*.

Have you ever seen the movie, "Groundhog
Day" starring Bill Murray and Andie

MacDowell? It's an early nineties movie about karma, self-reflection and personal growth. Murray plays Phil Connors, an arrogant Pittsburgh television weatherman who during an assignment covering the annual Groundhog Day event in Punxsutawney, Pennsylvania, finds himself caught in a time loop, repeating the same day again and again. After indulging in hedonism and committing suicide numerous times (in funny ways, not gory at all), he begins to re-examine his life and priorities.

At the core of the movie is selflessness. Murray, as Phil Connors, starts off as a narcissist who has one thing on his mind, finishing his assignment and leaving town. This is because this is his 4$^{th}$ year in a row going to Punxsutawney to cover the Groundhog event and he is focused on leaving the news station for bigger and better. Before heading to Punxsutawney, Phil is told that this trip is an opportunity to meet new people and see new things. But Phil is not amenable to growth. He arrives in Punxsutawney only concerned about what people are going to think of him and not the potential for change.

Any of this sound familiar? Passing the Bar and ultimately being a lawyer is not about you. It's about becoming a person that can put your client's best interest first (Thank you Ron Castro). If this is your third, fourth or fifth time taking the Bar, enter your next study session with an open-mind ready for change and personal growth. Take your ego and self-loathing out of the process. Erase from your mind any concerns about what others think about you. Think about your future employment opportunities and go into your study plan ready to become a more caring and thoughtful person.

On the first day in the movie, the Groundhog reveals that there will be six more weeks of winter. Phil's broadcast of the event is sarcastic, dry and crass. He just can't wait to leave and move on to more glamorous work. On his way out of town, he's stopped by a blizzard. Earlier in the movie he'd predicted the blizzard would not come, but ultimately, he is forced back to Punxsutawney. This was me the first two times I took the Bar. I was focused on my future as a lawyer litigating cases. I my dream was to be in a fast-paced career and balancing heavy workloads as a public defender. I couldn't see the value in what was right in front of me. I'd even told myself that I could just keep taking the Bar and I would pass without having to change anything, failure was only a fluke and moving on was just a matter of time.

Upon his return from the broadcast, Rita (Andie McDowell) invites Phil to the Groundhog dinner. Unbeknownst to Phil this is an opportunity to meet the townspeople, experience their culture and learn more about the groundhog tradition. Foolishly, Phil refuses to attend the dinner and the loop begins. If you recall, Phil was told once in the beginning of the movie that the trip's true purpose was to meet people. He was given a second chance before the loop began (the dinner). But his narrow mindedness and arrogance kept him from the very thing he wanted the most.

When the loop starts, it takes Phil awhile to recognize the cues. At first, he chalks it up to déjà vu. On the second day of the loop it hits him, and he frantically tracks down Rita and tries to explain to her what's happing to him. She, of course, is confused and does not believe nor understand what he is experiencing. Recognizing the loop is the first step in ending it. But to see it, you must be humble enough to know that change is necessary.

At the out-set Phil seeks professional help, first a doctor then a psychiatrist but neither can help him. Phil has yet to look to himself for the solution. This can happen to us also, we think that taking the perfect prep-course is the path to success, however, no prep-course can prepare you to pass if you are not ready to commit the time and effort that is required. Next, Phil begins to question why this day is repeating. The stress overcomes him and he becomes reckless and attempts suicide to stop the loop. But, after killing himself he just wakes up in the morning in the same hotel bed with the radio playing Sonny and Cher's, "I got you babe" and the day starts over. We can analogize Phil's suicide attempts to quitting the test. But just like Phil, you can't quit. There is something that lingers inside you that will not allow you to give up on yourself.

Overtime, Phil can predict pitfalls during his normal course of the day and is able to avoid stepping in pot holes and interacting with annoying townspeople. He soon realizes that the loop just won't stop so he indulges in sweets, cigarettes and eventually lusts after Nancy Taylor (an ancillary character) and then Rita. Phil has replaced his selfish desire for fame with sex. Again, the similarities ring true, there was a point when I replaced my desire to practice law with just a desire to pass the Bar, I only focused on passing and nothing else.

But only focusing on passing was too narrow minded for the time. I should have been focused on doing my best in practice and becoming a better person. After having sex with Nancy, Phil realizes that he really wants Rita. He wants her so much so that he forgets his preoccupation with the loop and spends his energy on trying to be the perfect man for Rita. He begins to probe her for private information day after day, memorizing her interests, secrets and desires to seduce her. We can also fall into this trap of trying to memorize exactly what the Bar wants in hopes of passing. You may achieve a passing score with this method, but it is not optimal for practicing law in the future. What you want is what Phil eventually turned to once all else failed, self-reflection accompanied by giving selflessly and focusing on being a better person overall.

Phil pursues Rita for the duration of the movie, learning a host of things about Rita including her love of French poetry, rocky road ice cream and sweet vermouth, yet even after all his efforts he cannot get her to sleep with him. In some scenes, his courting her come across as contrived and phony because it's all mimicking what Rita wants on the surface. Eventually he does come very close to sleeping with Rita until he tells her he loves her in haste. She knows this is untrue because they have only spent one day together. (For Phil, it's been years upon years). During the dialogue Rita exclaims that he can't love her because he only loves himself, to which Phil replies, "That's not true, I don't even like myself." Here, the movie reveals to us what we must know in-order to pass the Bar. We must learn to like ourselves. So how does Phil ever learn to like himself?

After countless unsuccessful attempts Phil gives up on trying to sleep with Rita. He becomes reenchanted with the loop and goes mad. He kidnaps the ground hog in a pickup truck and drives the truck off a cliff ending in a spectacular explosion. Over the next couple of loops Phil tries every way imaginable to commit suicide, but to no avail he keeps waking up without a scratch on him. Realizing that he cannot die, Phil explains to Rita that he is a God. He takes Rita around the diner where they meet every day and begins to recount intimate details about the customers like a psychic.

This scene is very important in our journey because it characterizes what happens after you take and study for the Bar multiple times without the correct mindset. Phil has learned everything about the townspeople, but it was not because he wanted to or saw the value in it. He knew so much about them because he'd spent so much time in the loop he could not help but to know everything. You can spend countless hours, days, weeks, months even years studying, you will learn everything you need to know, but may still not pass. Even after Phil professed his knowledge of the towns people he was still not let out of the loop.

It's not until Phil stops lusting after Rita, obsessing over ending the loop and begins to appreciate the town, its people and himself does he begin on the path to seeing another day. Phil takes up, piano, ice sculpting and even tries time and time again to save a homeless man from dying. He cannot save the old man no matter how hard he tries and learns that no matter what you do, you cannot change what it meant to be. He saves a young boy from falling out of a tree. He helps a group of ladies with their flat tire and saves the mayor from choking on a steak. He then uses the skills he learned in piano to treat the town to a performance during the Groundhog Day dinner.

By the end of the movie, Phil has learned that he must humbly focus on himself and seek self-improvement in the spirit of helping others. With that mind-set, you can study for the Bar and pass! At the Groundhog Day dinner Phil is approached and thanked by key characters in the movie for his good deeds and character. He is now tightly knit to the Punxsutawney community. At the end of the movie, there is an auction for charity where Rita places the highest bid for Phil. He has finally gotten what he wanted without trying; Rita has come to him instead of him chasing her. Phil has come full circle and the loop is finally broken.

Are you in a Groundhog loop? What is your major focus or purpose when you study? What can you do to be a better person in-order to break your loop?

As Shakespeare once wrote, "parting is such sweet sorrow." I hope that reading this book energizes you and gives you another perspective on taking the Bar. Remember that you are not alone and that you can pass this exam. There is light at the end of the tunnel and once you reach the light be prepared to enter a whole new world of challenges, defeats and exhilarating victories. The next section includes select diary entries I wrote during my time studying, taking and passing the Bar. They are evidence of my vulnerability, strength and perseverance. It was therapeutic to write a diary and I recommend you do the same. With that I say farewell, peace and blessings.

# SELECTED DIARY ENTRIES

9/18/2007

It seems that I always have my head in my ass. In other words, I'm unchangeably distracted. I'm uninterested in everything. It seems that I have no passion for anything. I have no causes. What once was my cause has now dissolved. I guess I was just dedicated to the "struggle" proving to myself that I could accomplish something. Maybe I thought others would see and I could be a role model. My train of thought has been derailed I'm headed toward a destitute destination. Boredom Ville population one.

Where is my fire? Where is my motivation to give Law school more, my ALL!!!!! I am sleepishly tired of being exhausted. I need a second wind. An alternate breeze will do. It's funny, when did I become the guy with no social life? Recently I haven't been able to keep a friend. Where are my hangout buddies?

Back to the lesson at hand. Perfection is expected so ima let em understand. Oh yeah, my motivation. What keeps me going? My family. The principle of finish what you start. To see the end of this particular challenge. Will things really be different? I could be an excellent attorney. The question is will I find my passion in this field?  In order for me to be my best I must be passionate.

What I think I need is time off.  Time off where I don't have a daunting task hanging over my head like.......... Finish law school, pass the Bar, get a job,,,,, so you can provide for your kids.  I did take on a lot without thinking.  I assumed that my skin was not flesh but some soft metallic alloy.  Did I have kids too early?  Dedicate myself to one woman too early?  What made me think I was so smart?  Like I knew everything and had my life all figured out.  I mean, the ship aint sunk by no means but we're drifting and I'm tired of rowing.

9/25/07

The Law of Attraction.  You become what you think about most.  You attract what you think about most.  Thoughts become things.  Thoughts have frequency.  Magnetism.  The Law of Attraction is obedient.  It manifests whatever you are thinking, positive or not.  What you think about you bring about.  Affirmative thoughts are more powerful than negative thoughts.  There is a time delay. Whatever you are thinking and feeling today creates your future.  Shifting awareness.

God's Plan

God wants you to take the money you get and do "business" to make more money. Investments (The internet). Use money to make money. Give money a job. Take Smart Calculated Risks. TSCR, Own land, physical, virtual. What about my dreams? God wants you to achieve your dreams. Can only be done with His timing.

• If you must force it to make it work, it's out of timing
• It should flow and come right on time. It should stay within your pace
• Go with the current

6/15/08

The next month and a half determines a lot. LA?, I will pass the Bar the 1$^{st}$ time. Attorney? Business? Politics? Not the 1$^{st}$ or 2$^{nd}$ time....

5/14/10

Funny that the last entry ends on the question of me passing the Bar the 1$^{st}$ 2$^{nd}$ or 3$^{rd}$ time. Needless to say I do not pass the 3$^{rd}$ time either. At this point it's not about taking the test. I've taken it 3 times prepared for it 3 times it's not as if I can't do it again. It's a matter of paying for the test and a new set of materials also my lap top is 5 years old and been through 3 Bars I don't know if it will make it.......

What's worse is the cabin fever and purgatory. If anything causes me to quit it will be those 2 factors. I can no longer be in the apartment, I can no longer just focus on the test. I need to move on regardless......... I've got to have other things going on.

At this point the day of failure for the 3$^{rd}$ time I don't know how to feel. It doesn't feel good but It really doesn't feel like the end of the world either. I just can't stand the loneliness. I'm going to put the Bar in 2$^{nd}$ place. My sanity is my first priority. I can't be worried about paying for this test. I am officially burnt out on this whole lawyer "dream" pursuit. It's funny how it seems that some have just moved on. I am however having a lot of trouble getting over this. I can't pin point what it is that I'm lacking. I guess it doesn't feel so bad because I can honestly say I gave it my all. I will retool and take it again. Brian said I never give up. I can't make him out to be a liar. I'll take the test again But I need to do something else too so that I don't go fucking nuts. This time around I will seek out more help.

7/19/10

I am growing, I am gaining more understanding. I was feeling that since I wasn't making money then I was not progressing, however, I have come to realize something. Making money is not an accurate measure for growth. How do I measure success? Here is the thing. I'm learning, I'm observing, I'm taking notes of what changes I need to make and I am even actively making those changes. Yet I've been feeling like I haven't been accomplishing anything because I'm not seeing an immediate substantial financial profit from my effort.

This feeling is naïve and it is becoming more clear what I am to do now. At this point I am training/preparing myself for the time when I will be out in the field. I don't need to be making money right now. I need to be preparing for my upcoming chapter/ the next "stage" in my career. Attorney/Musician/Entrepreneur

I'm growing because I've changed. And I'm making the changes that I suggested I should make.

1. Competitiveness
2. Being more open to approaching strangers
3. Cold calls
4. Heightened concern for quality of work
5. Improved work ethic

There is a change I want to make....... I want a heightened desire to be the best at whatever I'm doing. I should want to be the best. (do the best that I can do)

7/21/11

I will not lie on these pages. I do feel somewhat depressed. Today I found out that Brian W. has died. I don't know but for some reason I remember certain people. We were not close friends by any means but I can't help but feel sad about the loss. Moreover Brian's death puts my current situation into another perspective.

You see I was sad because I've spent the last, let's just say 3 years, attempting to pass the CA state Bar. It's not only that but for whatever reason, I can't seem to do anything else. I can't get involved in any other endeavors, job/hobby.

However, seeing how fragile life is changes my attitude. In short I could be gone, with No opportunity at all. It is difficult not to imagine that everyone has moved on and everyone is working, making money which gives them options. I spend lots of time in the house. But I do get to teach the girls the importance of diligent study. On this next attempt I'll be paying a tutor. Likely Bar passers.

I'm determined to give all 3 sections my full effort in preparation. I have no fear. I will not hold back. I will not allow any person or circumstance to distract me. I must admit, I am anxious for a guide during this next preparation season. My work ethic is stronger than ever. I must remember to keep practicing until I see results under time pressure.

R.I.P Brian Williams. Your passing reminds me of when T.J. Albrecht passed. Just out of nowhere. Death shows up once in a while. Reminding me of my mortality and how really insignificant the problems I whine about are.

From Aug – Jan: Prepare mentally for the Bar prep.

1. Stay positive
2. Stay focused
3. Make calculated moves
4. Enjoy the holidays
5. Rest
6. Think about technical aspects of the Bar
7. Forgive yourself

* Realize that you have another opportunity to realize your long-term goal and once that goal is achieved all this will instantly be a memory. The memory will be a testimony of your endurance/persistence/experience that you will share with others for their benefit.

9/18/14

I've passed the Bar. Got sworn in. Met a lot of new people. I'm working. I'm pushing myself to new heights. I feel like I'm getting closer to the place I've always known I could go. Still not there yet. I wonder what it will be like once I'm content/satisfied with my habits/mindset/behaviors/tendencies. Will I ever be satisfied? I like being comfortable with what I say or do no matter how it comes out, incorrect, not so polished or perfect.

I still have tons of ambition and still think writing straight to the point is the most comfortable for me. But, I do want to write more. Quality vs. Quantity? I'm getting better, but the process is so slow and it's hard to see improvement on a daily basis. You have to try hard and push for a while then look back and you will see the difference.

12/21/16

I'm an attorney in the field. I've been to trial. I've represented misdemeanor and felony clients. I've put on a live musical performance. I'm close to finishing the book. I'm still pushing hard, tightening up more than ever. I'm still not satisfied. I've become more financially educated. I am my own man. There are still ups and downs. Confident days and insecure days.

# SPECIAL THANKS

I'd like to thank GOD and all the people who have supported me throughout my journey in becoming an attorney. I cannot thank everyone but rest assured if your name is not mentioned I greatly appreciate you.

Firstly to my wife, Brieann Howard for our beautiful children and supporting us during my time in law school and taking the Bar. I love you. To my kids for bringing me happiness. To my Grandmother Lois Beason for providing a safe home. To my mother Theresa Beason for teaching me to be different and kind to others. To my aunt Flora Williams for teaching me to be smart with money, showing me how to run a business and giving me those extra treats that make me feel special. To my uncle Joseph Fields for showing me that I'm better than my mistakes. To my Father, Curtis Howard for telling me that, "everything is happening the way it's supposed to." To my aunt Cheryl Williams for coming through in the clutch. To my aunt Denise Beason for being a spiritual guide through the tough times.

To my mentors and colleagues. Thanks to Professor William Dillon of California State University Sacramento for ushering me into the world of Constitutional Law. Alesa Schachter for inviting me into her home. Alvin Gittisriboongul for inviting me to play basketball with some great guys. To John Woodall for your guidance in my first job in the legal field as a courier. Jacques Whitfield for being a good role model. Dr. Stan Oden aka Stan the man, you already know brother. The Chief Clerk of the California State Assembly E. Dotson Wilson thank you for believing that I would ultimately succeed. Brian Ebbert still the coolest guy I know. Moira Delgado and Sharon Pinkney for believing that I was worthy of outreach.

To my brother Larry A. Webb, who taught me how to ski. To my brother Harvey Hughes for visiting me when I had a severe case of cabin fever. To the last class of the New College School of Law, we are a part of history. To Paul Pfau and Bob Hull for their guidance on the road to passing the Bar. To Keith Staten, for teaching me the basics of practicing criminal law in Sacramento. To Jim Warden my brother in Christ. To Michelle Spaulding and Patricia Campi for seeing something special in me and trusting me with a substantive caseload. To David Brown for reigniting my desire to play guitar. And to my good friend Ron Castro for paying it forward and helping me become a more confident attorney. ALL GLORY TO GOD.